FINANCIAL FREEDOM
in a
THUMB DRIVE

The Millennial's Guide to Building Passive Income Online

KURT ROSWELL

If you purchase this book without a cover, you should be aware that this book may have been stolen property and reported as "unsold and destroyed" to the publisher. In such case, neither the author nor the publisher has received any payment for this "stripped book."

This publication is designed to provide competent and reliable information regarding the subject matter covered. However, it is sold with the understanding that the author and publisher are not engaged in rendering legal, financial, or other professional advice. Laws and practices often vary from state to state and country to country, and if legal or other expert assistance is required, the services of a professional should be sought. The author and publisher specifically disclaim any liability that is incurred from the use or application of the contents of this book.

Financial Freedom in a Thumb Drive

Printed and Published by:
Central Book Supply, Inc.
927 Phoenix Building, Quezon Ave., Quezon City

ISBN: 978-621-02-0831-3

Cover design: Elaine Samonte

First Edition

Foreword

It is my life's mission to help change peoples' lives positively. It is a calling born out of my life struggles. After digging myself out of poverty to become a successful businesswoman, I gained a deeper appreciation for the profound impact financial freedom has on a person's life. I have since nurtured a passion for helping ordinary people realize their extraordinary potential.

That same passion drove me to be a best-selling author, an international speaker, a world traveler, and an entrepreneur. My greatest trials became the building blocks that placed me in the company of remarkable individuals – like Jack Canfield, Mark Victor Hansen, Robert Kiyosaki, Wayne Dyer, T Harv Eker, and Brian Tracy – who have touched so many lives.

The most powerful gifts are those we forge from the deepest struggles. My passion was forged this way. Likewise, Kurt fought through his obstacles and came out with a powerful gift of his own.

An unassuming Millennial I met at one of my seminars, Kurt overcame multiple failures on his way to financial freedom. His disappointments gifted him with unparalleled precision and attention to detail for his methodologies, something that can only come from firsthand trial and error. For a step-by-step Millennial's guide to financial freedom and building passive income online, there is no one better equipped to serve as your usher on this journey of yours.

Financial Freedom in a Thumb Drive is an essential tool for this Millennial generation fueled by its creativity, imagination, and wonder, yet burdened by the financial realities of the modern world. Starting out with negligible resources is always the most impossible part of pursuing financial freedom. This book just made it more possible for you – by moving financial freedom within the reach of every Millennial, regardless of starting point.

I have no doubt that Kurt, and this book, belong in that same category of remarkable individuals who will change the lives of many people. Read this book, take it into practice, and one of those changed lives will be yours.

Jhet van Ruyven
Best-Selling Author, "The Tale of Juliet"
Mentor & Entrepreneur
International Speaker
http://www.jhetvanruyven.com/

To all my fellow Millennials, it's our time.

Contents

Chapter 1
The Turn of the Millennium, The Turn of the Millennials

Financial Freedom for Millennials

"You weren't born just to pay bills and die."
– Anonymous

The Color of Freedom: Appreciate the Benefits of Financial Freedom

I never thought I'd love the color blue so much.

Some 6.5 miles up in the air, I was fortunate enough to get a window seat – all the better to enjoy the view on my plane ride home. The sight of the vast blue sky and the white clouds scudding through it took me back to the unforgettable time I'd just finished enjoying.

The clouds reminded me of the pearly-white sand and sea foam that served as "border patrol," frisking my feet before allowing them entry into the soothing saltwater. After that, there was only blue infinity. Without a doubt, the place I was flying away from was the most gorgeous place I'd ever visited thus far.

The term "feeling blue" may mean sadness for most people. I, on the other hand, enjoyed a different tone of blue during that moment – the blue shade of freedom.

Romantic recollections aside, I was flying home from a fun-filled vacation with seven of my wonderful friends. We'd just enjoyed an adventure filled with firefly-watching, partying, island-hopping, snorkeling, kayaking, beer tasting, and plenty of good eats. The entire journey spanned the friendly city of Puerto Princesa and the untainted paradise of El Nido – both places highlighting the beauty, love, and hospitality of Palawan, Philippines.

This trip I'm talking about is nothing out of the ordinary. Groups of family and friends go on vacation adventures all the time. Palawan is already a well-known tourist destination. What made this particular trip interesting for me were the circumstances that surrounded it. Context, after all, is what makes any tale worth telling.

Let me explain.

I booked the trip a year in advance. It was a spontaneous decision I made without much thought, worry, or planning. One late night a year earlier, I got a call from a friend asking me to join his leisure trip to Palawan. He'd already booked his flight. He gave me his flight itinerary and off I went online to buy my plane ticket. I gave no thought to the cost of the ticket, nor did I hesitate to worry about possible conflicts with my work schedule on those dates.

Someone extended an invitation, and I felt like going. So I went. That's it. I made this decision without overthinking. My unique financial situation afforded me such indulgence.

Fortune smiled on us, too – the tickets were on sale. All of us ended up with more pocket money for the escapade. It didn't escape my attention though that a few of my trip buddies were working within a budget. Not all, but a few, would pass on the more expensive activities, while others were very particular about where we would eat, citing budget concerns.

In contrast, I jumped into every adventure. It felt great looking at the items on the left side of the menu and picking what I wanted, instead of concerning myself with the right side and doing mental math on what I could afford.

For those who didn't have to worry about their budgets, the schedule was a bigger issue. The whole trip spanned a Friday morning to a Wednesday night. Four from our group had to cut their vacations short to fly back to their jobs and businesses.

I got to enjoy the full ride.

It was also during this trip that I fully appreciated the freedom of being able to follow my heart, instead of doing "calendar *Jenga*" around a busy work schedule – all the while praying that my "real" life wouldn't fall apart while I was out having fun.

During that getaway, I also saw that work responsibilities followed all of my friends to Palawan. Every so often, someone had to excuse himself or herself to take a call or email a client. Only the beach and lagoon parts of the vacation (where cell reception was hit and miss) provided much-needed breathing space.

I received zero interruptions. I was able to live in every moment and take pleasure in every second of that journey, worry-free. I didn't have to deal with constant disruptions that would have spoiled the experience.

This experience is just one example of what having financial freedom has done for me – I can be present in the moment, at the location of the experience, instead of having my mind dragged back to work.

Financial freedom allowed me to break through the cap of my earning potential. Since then, I managed to quadruple the amount I made from my last corporate job as an Online Marketing Director. If I want more, I have the power to increase my monthly income by contributing more to the world – not having to wait (or beg) for a salary increase dictated by my employer.

Financial freedom granted me the free time to recharge and recover. I take vacations or rest days whenever I need (or want) it, even on regular weekdays. If I catch a bug, I have the luxury of taking my time to recover and get back to full health – secured with the fact that I control my time and my businesses would continue to grow in my absence.

Financial freedom afforded me the choice to follow what I want and pursue what's important for me. I can attend a valued friend's wedding on a weekday or commit to an afternoon get together on a whim. If I want to follow a long-unrealized passion, I can do so without pressure or guilt – I can proceed with any life-changing decision without the need for permission, compromise, or selling out.

Financial freedom offers many benefits, and I am thankful for the blessings that brought me to this point where I enjoy every one of those benefits. It sounds like an amazing experience now, but how I got to this point is a tad less glamorous story.

Living in a Baby-Booming World: Integrating the Millennial Generation

Saying that I am a Millennial seems like as good a starting point for the story of my journey as any. There are no precise dates for when the Millennial generation starts or ends, but the expert consensus places Millennials as people born between the 1980s and early 2000s.

The Millennial generation accounts for 92 million people in the United States alone, and two billion globally. That's a staggering number of people that covers more than one-fourth of the world's population today.

Baby Boomers, on the other hand, make up the generation of our parents. Again, there are no precise dates, and this is a loose definition (Gen X and Xennials be damned). However, for our purposes, experts define Baby Boomers as persons born between 1946 and 1964, just after the Second World War.

At 76 million strong in the U.S. during their time, the Baby Boomers comprise a smaller number than our Millennial generation does. Despite this, our parents' generation is a major influence in the world we live in today. It's easy to see that the world's biggest corporations and the most powerful political positions are filled with and controlled by Baby Boomers. In terms of money, at least, Baby Boomers are the wealthiest generation in history.

In other words, my fellow Millennials, we may have strength in numbers, but we are operating in *their* arena. We are the away team coming in to play in the Baby Boomers' home turf. Just like any team protecting their home court against invaders, the Baby Boomers have formed a scathing opinion of Millennials. At the very least, the previous generation finds Millennial attitudes, cultures, and values very confusing.

Clint Eastwood, the legendary actor and director, in an interview with Esquire magazine, called the Millennials as a *weak* generation – using a more provocative term I prefer not to dignify with repetition.

Ron Alsop, a known business journalist and author, dubbed the Millennials as *trophy kids* – a generation of kids that grew up receiving trophies and medals for simply participating, whom then grew up into "the most demanding and the most coddled generation in history."

Simon Sinek, an author, motivational speaker, and marketing consultant, tore the Millennial generation a new one in a video interview about *Millennials in the Workplace*. In that video that went viral, Mr. Sinek illustrated in detail the Millennial generation's sense of entitlement, itch for instant gratification, and addiction to technology.

In all honesty, who can blame them for these perceptions?

Our generation underscores a mad scramble for *likes*, *shares*, *comments*, and going viral. We hit a new low with that *Tide Pod Challenge*, fam. Important matters of meaning and substance take a backseat on our priorities.

How about our generation's strongest foundation for making decisions – the #YOLO? Have you ever justified a risky, ill-advised, or downright stupid decision using this four-letter acronym? These bad decisions dig Millennials into very deep holes, often financially, which are very hard to escape.

I suspect most readers have already entertained several distractions on their way reading up to this point – we're just in the half mark of Chapter 1, BTW. Our generation suffers from short attention spans – we constantly shift across multiple screens and rely on *tl;dr* (too long; didn't read) versions of content to function properly. This general lack of concentration and focus is clawing away at our productivity, effectiveness, and potential.

These shreds of evidence may suggest that our Baby Boomer predecessors' critical view of our Millennial generation is well-substantiated. However, our generation may simply hold different values from those cherished by the Baby Boomer generation. We probably see and do things differently as digital technology natives. We don't go through life the same way our parents did. We also don't measure material success the way our parents do.

It's not necessarily better or worse, just different. I'll give us big props on one key aspect though – the Millennial generation's ability to adapt and explore is second to none. We gladly try every new device and intuitively know how to use new technology. We can quickly learn additional skills and vocations beyond our main career track. This flexibility will serve us well as we move into and through a fast-changing and unpredictable future.

Why is it essential to have a clear view of the attitudes, culture, and values of the Millennial generation? As of 2015, Millennials officially became the largest generation in the U.S. labor force. Millennials are also influencing the U.S. economy and affecting established industries along the way.

Soon, other countries will follow. Millennials will be the dominant force that shapes the world's future. With that, we also embody a large group of people striving and in dire need of financial freedom.

The Baby Boomers presume that we are failing as a generation. Millennials, on the other hand, feel that we are being told to follow an outdated approach that doesn't fit today's fast-paced world. Only time will tell which generation is right.

In my case, I was fortunate to choose a path that led me to financial freedom. This freedom is what I want to share with you, people of my generation.

Freedom is the Operative Word: Know the Four Stages of Financial Freedom

When people hear the term financial freedom, the first idea that comes to mind is money. The phrase starts with the word *finance*, after all. Thus, it sends the entire working population into a rat race to earn as much income as possible, regardless of the effect on their health, their relationships, and their sanity.

Realize that the real operative word on that phrase is *freedom*. We "work to live" not "live to work," after all. Achieving genuine financial freedom merits more consideration than just earning as much as we can.

Money is necessary – we can't pay bills, eat, or have a place to live without earning it. However, it's only a single element in the entire financial freedom equation. Let me share the four stages of financial freedom to give you a more complete picture.

Stage 1: Financial dependence

All of us start at this stage. When I was born, I was incapable of fending for myself. My parents provided for my needs. I was dependent.

My dependence to my parents obliged me to listen to their words and follow their instructions, lest they decide to stop caring for me. I may know, deep down, that my parents love me, but I dare not contradict their directives and test the limits of their love. Putting it bluntly, I was at my parents' mercy – for food, clothing, education, shelter, and care.

I believed that my financial dependence would end the day I get a job, start earning my own money, and pay for my own expenses. Independence is the fruit of #adulting, right? Well, not really.

After graduating from college, I was fortunate to find a good job situation. I enjoyed my work. Starting my corporate career as a Store Manager for a well-known company right out of college was nice. I earned a good paycheck, had the respect of my constituents, and a challenging environment that fueled my growth. However, I soon realized that while I was no longer dependent on my parents, my financial dependence shifted to my employer.

The essence of this financial dependence is the same. We must follow the orders of our employer if we want to keep receiving paycheck money. The only difference is that with an employer, love is not part of the equation – work is. That still makes us financially dependent. We are now at the mercy of our employer – for our salary, promotion, tasks, and even vacation days.

Changing companies and jobs won't solve any of these financial dependence issues, either. We Millennials love job-hopping, thinking this will bring us financial freedom. Employment is still employment. The arrangement is the same wherever we end up. Some work environments are simply more comfortable or tolerable than others.

We can only gain true financial independence by breaking out of employment and learning to earn money outside corporate shackles.

Stage 2: Financial independence

I decided to take some freelance projects while working as a full-time employee. I know a bit of Photoshop, so I took on simple graphics work. They were easy enough to get into, and I worked on those projects during my spare time.

I felt liberated to have another stream of income. I also felt more secure because I was no longer dependent on a single point of failure (i.e., my employer) for my finances. More importantly, taking on freelance projects allowed me to break through my earnings cap – an income ceiling dictated by my boss.

When we have control over the amount of money we can make, we have gained **money freedom** to become financially independent. Whether via freelancing, commission-based sales, or running our own business, the essence of financial independence is the ability to dictate our own income.

Most people stop at financial independence thinking that it's the same as financial freedom. It isn't, and I didn't.

I realized that while I am in control of how much money I make, my earnings always follow the amount of time I can provide. It's a "no work, no pay" arrangement, despite the pay being potentially high. I recognized soon enough that I have limited time – just like everyone else.

Gaining **money freedom** is a good start – it opens up more options for us. However, **money freedom** alone is not enough to achieve true financial freedom. We need to learn how to generate income that is not directly dependent on the hours or effort that we put in.

Stage 3: Financial freedom

I started exploring even more avenues for earning money. I attended trade expos, joined entrepreneur groups, read business books, and enrolled in business seminars. It's amazing how many financial opportunities become available to us if we just open our eyes and look a little closer.

Along the way, I tried several ventures, like participating in sales bazaars, selling items online, stock trading, and even joining a Network Marketing company. The results of my explorations varied from losing money to earning a bit more than my original investment.

My most important insight from experience is this – not all income opportunities are equal. From that realization, I was able to draw out the key component that leads to true financial freedom.

When we can keep generating income independent of our presence or time (i.e., while sleeping), we have gained the **time freedom** to become financially free. When enough cash flow is automatically generated to cover the cost of our lifestyle, then we can take our leave from having to work physically for the foreseeable future. This is the essence of true financial freedom.

From that financially free platform, I now have the freedom to learn any skill, do any activity, and pursue any interest – even if it's outside of my field. Money comes in without my direct efforts, and my schedule is left wide open.

Financial freedom gave me the liberty to write this book without worry or pressure. If I chose to write this on a beautiful beach somewhere on a Wednesday afternoon, that was perfectly possible too.

While I am now financially free, I'm not yet rich. Yes, there's a difference.

There is still a stage beyond financial freedom. Having control over my money and time, I realized that it's time for me to work on financial abundance.

Stage 4: Financial abundance

It's amazing how achieving financial freedom can take some of life's major worries away. I'm secure that my cash flow can maintain my modest way of life and cover my needs. I'm also liberated from following an abusive work schedule that is dictated by a boss. However, I am not yet rich, nor am I financially abundant.

There's a fine line between *rich* and *financially abundant*, but knowing the difference can have a huge impact on your financial journey. Let me explain.

Timothy Ferriss said that "$1,000,000 in the bank isn't the fantasy. The fantasy is the lifestyle of complete freedom it supposedly allows." The rich aren't necessarily financially free or abundant, and the financially free don't need to be filthy rich.

Rich is a superficial display measured solely by how much money one has or how much stuff one owns. For those who want to be more precise, *rich* describes a person with high net worth. *Rich* doesn't include the criteria of having control over one's income (e.g., rich because of inheritance or lottery) or having free time to enjoy life (e.g., rich but overworked).

Financial abundance involves achieving financial freedom – having **money freedom** and **time freedom** – but going beyond to a point where lavish, erroneous, or altruistic financial decisions have a negligible impact on one's financial standing.

When we can make any financial decision – wise or unwise – with no risk, harm, or burden to our way of life, we have gained **choice freedom**. Short of defying physical limitations, breaking the realm of possibilities, and violating moral and legal standards, we are free to pursue any choice or decision we want.

I am financially free. However, I still need to be careful about the decisions I make. I can't yet donate a huge chunk of my resources to charity as Bill Gates can. I'm incapable yet of going out and finding a solution to humanity's energy consumption problem like Elon Musk is doing. I still can't spend my disposable income on shiny watches, fancy cars, big yachts, and private jets like social media sensation Dan Bilzerian does.

I still need to make smart choices to continue growing my financial condition or risk losing my financial freedom. I'm not yet financially abundant.

Financial freedom is an important goal to work hard for. It changes your life and opens up your options. Once you get there though, aim for the freedom to do whatever you want and spend your resources as you see fit, without risking your financial freedom. That is the dream – financial abundance.

Goal set. Let's begin with our adventure.

Financial Freedom for Millennials: Wrap-Up and Pro Tips

The world is changing, but our ideals and decisions keep clinging to old habits. Why do we keep blindly following the financial path of previous generations when we know that those ideas are no longer enough for today's fast-paced world? This quote from Robert Kiyosaki might hold the answer – "The fear of being different prevents most people from seeking new ways to solve their problems."

In this Information Age, there is an abundance of opportunities beyond the employment path – financial avenues that lead to genuine financial freedom.

The attitudes, cultures, and values of the Millennial generation are aligned to capitalize on these opportunities, more so than any previous generation. Financial freedom is within reach of every Millennial – now more than ever.

Understand that when it comes to financial freedom, *freedom* is the operative word. We can't be financially free by earning money alone, no matter how large the salary may get. *Rich* is not equal to *financially free*.

To move upward through the different stages of financial freedom, we need to work on securing three freedoms.

Getting **money freedom** moves us from financial dependence to financial independence. **Money freedom** allows us to earn income that is not based on our salary but based on our worth.

Securing **time freedom** moves us from financial independence to financial freedom. **Time freedom** releases us from the situation of being constantly pressed for time. Instead, we run a schedule that highlights control over our time.

Achieving **choice freedom** moves us from financial freedom to financial abundance. **Choice freedom** frees us to make decisions not because we have to, but because we want to.

Remember that it is prudent to work on securing these freedoms in that order – money, then time, then choice. Doing otherwise can lead to disastrous results. Imagine quitting your job and going full #YOLO. Doing so frees up our time and choice, but we won't get far without money to support us.

Knowing now what genuine financial freedom is and how accessible it is to any Millennial, where does building passive income online fit into the picture?

Chapter 2

Large Operation,
Tiny Thumb Drive

Passive Income Vehicles and Online Marketing

"Most people find that good advice they're given doesn't fit their comfort zone, so they blow it off. Get out of that zone!" – Blair Singer

The Way Out of This Rat Race: Recognize Passive Income

J ust like that, it's almost over.

The weekend went by so fast. The dread that comes at the close of each weekend settles in again. I count the hours before I need to wake up early, get back to the office, and slave at my job for another week. This is a familiar sentiment that all of us know way too well.

It's not like I hated my job. I loved the prestige of working for a reputable company. I enjoyed the respect I earned from colleagues and subordinates alike. I also thrived on the trials of the challenging environment set before me. I'm one of those lucky few who got paid well for doing work that I liked.

What I did hate was the daily grind aspects of the job that had little to do with my work output. I hated piling into rush hour traffic. I hated navigating through the rough waters of office politics. I hated missing important life events because my job took priority above all else.

I realized how much of a zero-sum game my corporate life was. I managed to secure a decent salary throughout my corporate journey. However, each paycheck comes eroded by taxes, mandatory contributions, and deductions for social safety nets, as well as work-related expenses like commute fares, eating out, and socializing with co-workers. How can anyone raise his or her standard of living off the crumbs of what's left after all these additional expenses?

Working a job is the living definition of a rat race – running hard but not going anywhere, just like a hamster in its exercise wheel. I suddenly had this deep-seated desire to break out of this corporate prison.

Charles Bukowski expressed the experience in his novel **Factotum** more bluntly – "How in the hell could a man enjoy being awakened at 6:30 a.m. by an alarm clock, leap out of bed, dress, force-feed, shit, piss, brush teeth and hair, and fight traffic to get to a place where essentially you made lots of money for somebody else and were asked to be grateful for the opportunity to do so?"

So harsh, but so true.

The core of my employment dread: Getting answers from a book

As fate would have it, the key out of that corporate prison came to me in the form of a book – Robert Kiyosaki's **Rich Dad Poor Dad**.

I first heard about that book when I was in college. A professor mentioned it in passing while giving us advice on how to succeed in life after graduation. I simply shrugged it off at the time because it didn't seem relevant to my studies.

A year later, a trusted friend of mine brought the book up while we were discussing career plans. He said reading that book would change my life. My friend wasn't kidding. I finished the book in two reading sessions. Thus began the drastic change in the course of my career and financial life.

Rich Dad Poor Dad shared many insights about how money works that should be taught in our homes and schools, but aren't. The section on the essential distinction between assets vs. liabilities alone is invaluable. Many people can get out of their financial troubles by simply knowing the difference between those two things.

For my corporate slave situation, the way the book described the myth behind the idea of job security stood out even more. Our society perpetuates the idea that employment is the best way to gain a secure financial future, yet the book opened my eyes to the cruel reality.

Employment can only give an illusion of security via a predictable, scheduled paycheck – nothing more. In exchange for that predictability, I would have to give up the most productive years of my life building my boss's business and bottom line. I realized that trade leans heavily against my favor.

However, no realization from the book terrified me more than this one single idea – retirement. Regardless of our financial and career ideologies, we all have to face the inevitable moment of retirement – that point when we are no longer deemed capable of working.

The truth is, most people push away or, God forbid, ignore planning for retirement at their own peril. Then, they realize too late that the companies they gave the best years of their lives to won't care for them beyond their useful working days.

There was a time when companies took care of their employees after retirement. Back then, these companies continued to pay their retired employees' salaries and healthcare benefits for the rest of these employees' lives. In such cases, we can understand why employment leads to lifetime financial security.

Those days are long gone. Companies began to realize that it is expensive to continue paying employees who no longer work, who live long life spans, and who add no value to the company's bottom line. This practice is bad for business and business has adjusted to fix that.

The norm today is that once you retire, you get a lump sum amount based on your years of service. Then you have to fend for yourself for whatever remains of your life.

Let's face the hard truth – companies are not loyal to their employees. You hear the catchphrase "no one is indispensable" uttered in this light.

After getting hit with this ugly truth, I knew I needed to change my career trajectory. I needed to start working on getting out of the employment rat race.

Not all are created equal: Understand the three types of income

Rich Dad Poor Dad boldly pointed out the problem. Fortunately, it was also kind enough to reveal the solution. ***Rich Dad Poor Dad*** prepared the escape trail from employment prison by explaining the three different income types – **earned income**, **paper income**, and **passive income**.

Earned income is when we get paid for our labor and skill. This describes employment and freelancing.

Earned income also covers income sources that require our attention to keep generating income. Business owners who are critical cogs of their businesses fall under this category. In all of the mentioned cases, we are essentially exchanging our time and skills for money.

Paper income is income derived from selling any financial instrument or item of value at a higher price than we originally paid for it. It's essentially the same as **portfolio income** or **capital gain income**. It is called "paper income" because we don't get to realize the profits (or losses) until we sell the financial instrument or the valuable item. Until we cash it in, this type of income exists only "on paper."

Buying low and selling high on financial instruments like stocks, bonds, and derivatives, as well as valuable items like land, equipment, commodities, memorabilia, jewelry, and precious stones and metals all fall under the paper income umbrella.

Passive income is income generated by assets we build or possess. This does not come from a simple increase in the market price of an asset. The asset produces valuable output – products, services, interests, or dividends – that generate income and cash flow.

Assets give us income whether we work on it or not. Imagine a golden goose that lays golden eggs regularly and you get a picture of what passive income looks like.

Earned income is limited because all of us have limited time – 24 hours a day, seven days a week, 52 weeks a year. Also, when, for any reason (i.e., retirement, accident, illness), we are no longer able to work, the income stops – immediately.

Paper income, on the other hand, doesn't provide a consistent cash flow. Paper income is also dependent on market forces. Unfortunately, the market, if history is any indication, is always unpredictable and volatile.

My readings of **Rich Dad Poor Dad** revealed the single greatest truth when it comes to financial literacy, one that we have been building up to since you began reading this book – only passive income from assets can offer you true financial freedom.

It's time to explore our passive income options.

Not Tall Enough for the Roller Coaster: Facing the Four Classic Financial Freedom Vehicles

Do you know those height check signs on amusement park rides? Ever got rejected on those? I have. I was so excited to go on the Octopus ride way back when I was a kid. It was to be my very first thrill ride experience, but I was too young and too short for admittance to that ride.

In a sense, the start of my journey to building passive income was like that too.

When I read **Rich Dad Poor Dad**, I gained an amazing sense of financial clarity. Gaining financial literacy and learning how money works got me excited to go and build passive income. I was ecstatic to work on a financially free life. However, I was devastated to realize that I wasn't tall enough for that ride, metaphorically speaking.

My situation as a full-time employee and the resources I had back then made it difficult – borderline impossible – to successfully follow and execute any of the financial freedom vehicles enumerated in **Rich Dad Poor Dad**.

Let me elaborate.

Financial freedom vehicle 1: Real estate

Real estate investing sounded like a winner. Robert Kiyosaki and his "rich dad" built their fortunes via real estate. In **Rich Dad Poor Dad** terms, real estate investments mean owning property and renting them out for passive income.

When I considered my financial situation then though, I didn't have enough capital to get into real estate investments of that sort. I was just learning about financial literacy then. Was I willing to take on loans, mortgage my limited assets, and play a dangerous game with my credit in an industry that I still did not know well? Not really.

It's really hard for a full-time employee to engage in this type of real estate investment. The financial risks at that stage of my life were just too great. Maybe when I am more experienced and have a better grasp of how money works, I can reconsider investing in real estate to strengthen my financial freedom. Back then though, I was too short for that ride.

Financial freedom vehicle 2: Businesses

Building businesses, now that was interesting. Most of the wealthy and financially free people around the world are businesspeople, after all. Compared to real estate, businesses require significantly less capital to set up. A close friend and I were thinking of putting one up for a very long time. Maybe it was time to start.

Upon close inspection though, all businesses demand their owners' focused involvement during the start-up process. My friend and I weren't willing or confident enough to leave the safety of our full-time jobs then. We didn't have much business experience, either. Also, the well-known statistic saying that nine out of 10 businesses fail wasn't reassuring to either of us.

I still think businesses are great sources of income. But it wasn't possible for me to start building one <u>and still</u> work at my full-time job. It would have to be one or the other. I was not ready to make that leap of faith.

Financial freedom vehicle 3: Paper assets

Paper assets, stock trading, and foreign exchange (forex) trading – I like the sound of those words. Most of the world's money seems to grow out of Wall Street and the stock exchanges. Stock trading, in particular, is easy to get into. Brokers offer low investment thresholds, and trading fees continue to drop.

I opened an online account with a reputable broker's trading platform, got familiar with the interface, and executed some trades. Then I realized that stock trading doesn't consistently generate passive income. Dividends from holding stock don't come as often to be considered reliable income.

For a corporate employee, it's really easy to get into investing in paper assets. However, it's not a good place to start building my passive income stream. Paper assets work better for raising capital or preserving wealth, not achieving financial freedom.

Financial freedom vehicle 4: "The Perfect Business"

Finally came what Kiyosaki called "the perfect business" – Network Marketing, otherwise known as Multi-Level Marketing (MLM). This industry has low entry requirements and can be done while keeping my day job.

The business model allowed me to focus on the selling part – the products as well as the business opportunity – and growing my network. The company took care of the product manufacturing, development, and delivery as well as accounting, legal, and administrative work. My hopes were very high for this financial freedom vehicle.

It was a struggle at the start – with adjusting my schedule and learning the skills – but I managed to build a substantial network within a few months. My business grew, products were moving, and money was coming in. I began to understand why many people use Network Marketing to get out of the rat race. The longer I stayed though, the more I realized why this supposedly "perfect business" was not perfect for reaching my goal of financial freedom after all.

You see, Network Marketing is a "leading people" kind of business. The leaders or "uplines" – the people at the top – need to keep leading the new "downlines" – the people at the bottom – for the network to stay healthy and running. I realized this when I observed MLM veterans who had been in the company for more than a decade still working as actively as when they started.

The network of "downlines" would collapse from lack of leadership if the key "uplines" take long breaks, or worse, leave. I saw this happen to many groups within my MLM company, and the same happened to my network of "downlines" when I chose to pursue other interests. As my network collapsed, the passive income came crashing down with it.

Don't get me wrong, Network Marketing works as a business model. In essence, it's an "expanded franchising" model, where the royalty income extends beyond the first level of "franchisees." It remains one of the best and most accessible options for full-time corporate employees who want to break free of corporate bonds. I just can't see the pot of financial freedom gold at the end of the MLM rainbow.

All these financial freedom vehicles loom too big for a small first-timer, especially an <u>employed</u> beginner. I kept searching for the financial freedom vehicle that I am tall enough to ride. Eventually, I stumbled upon the passive income vehicle that fits my situation perfectly – one that is very accessible to corporate employees with little extra cash, restrictive schedules, and minimal experience.

As fate would have it, I would cross paths with a financial freedom vehicle that fits the palm of my hand – figuratively and literally.

A Financial Freedom Empire Fits in a Thumb Drive: Appreciate the Power of Making Money Online

In December of 2006, I opened up my **Yahoo! Mail** account to go through my daily emails. On this fateful day, a spam email caught my eye. The subject line had these words written on it – *Make Millions Online*. I got curious enough to open and read the email text.

The email had come from a nondescript email address, probably randomly generated, as most spammers do. It promoted an instructional book titled **Lucrative List Building – How Everyday People Are Building Huge, Highly Profitable Opt-In Email Lists from Scratch to Make Millions Online** by Glen Hopkins.

Back then, Hopkins' **Lucrative List Building** sold for the affordable price of $19, was in eBook format, and included resale rights. Resale rights give me the rights to sell the same product and keep 100% of the profits, as long as I do this without altering the product.

Imagine, an everyday person like me (as specified in the subtitle), can make millions online (also mentioned in the subtitle), and get started immediately with a product to sell (because of the resale rights) for only $19. It was a great deal, however way we cut it. Therefore, I went ahead and bought the product. The rest, as they say, is history.

Well, not really. I wish I could say that I made millions online off the bat, as **Lucrative List Building** promises in its subtitle. Sadly, the road toward online business success came long and hard for me.

I tried the methods the book described, but failed to make millions. It wasn't easy – but, then again, nothing is. However, **Lucrative List Building** piqued my interest enough about the potential of making money online that I was motivated to explore the subject further.

In May of 2007, I attended the **World Internet Megasummit** in Singapore. This event featured some of the world's most successful Online Marketers – a star-studded group which introduced a specific approach to making money online called Internet Marketing, or Online Marketing, that goes beyond selling services as a freelancer yet stopping short of building a full-blown Silicon Valley tech startup.

On that event, I saw an Online Marketer – Stephen Pierce – make \$100,000 in 3 days. I didn't understand much during that time, and mixed reviews have followed Pierce since. However, when Pierce showed the audience a newly created **PayPal** account with \$0.00 on the first day, and the same **PayPal** account with more than \$100,000 on the last day (via several small transactions from multiple sources), I saw the power of Online Marketing and making money online.

I was obsessed with learning all about Online Marketing – which involves making money completely online with no offline aspects, just a combination of skills, online services, and web platforms.

It took me 17 failures throughout four years of trying out different Online Marketing methods and putting up different websites before I hit my stride.

That was four years of trying and failing. I blew through thousands of dollars paying for courses, products, and services. I labored through hundreds of hours spent studying, building, writing, and executing online campaigns. I pushed through a barrage of hopeless feelings and self-doubts. Then, when I was about to give up, I finally built something that worked and made money online.

My first successful campaign involved a simple website on health and fitness that showed up well in **Google** for specific search terms – a practice called *Search Engine Optimization (SEO)*. The website contained informative content and earned money by selling other people's products for a percentage commission, in a setup known as an *affiliate* arrangement. I was able to build the website up until it consistently made a couple of thousand dollars each month.

It wasn't a campaign that would make me filthy rich, but it was a major confidence booster to finally experience consistent sales for myself. There's a difference between being able to cash in checks from my online venture instead of just reading about them. I finally tasted the sweet promise of online income that I could only see from a distance a few years ago.

That one successful campaign also paid for all of my past failures, recouped all my losses, and funded the online projects I embarked on after it. I have since built more online campaigns and diversified into other investments on the way to a financially free life.

My most important realization from that experience is this – in this digital age, the vehicle for financial freedom doesn't have to be a big, tangible asset. It doesn't have to be a large brick-and-mortar store frequented by a stream of foot-traffic customers. It doesn't have to be a fully-occupied apartment building. It doesn't have to be a substantial stake on a blue-chip company. It doesn't have to be a large room full of "downlines."

We have the option of building a passive income asset made of bits, bytes, and data that can fit in a small package – a thumb drive, also known as a flash drive or a USB drive. In this digital age, literally and figuratively, financial freedom is within reach and can sit in the palm of your hand.

Financial freedom for all: What Online Marketing can do for us

When I managed to jump from employment to financial freedom, I realized why Online Marketing trumps the classic passive income vehicles I mentioned earlier. This is especially true for Millennials who have full-time jobs. Here are the main advantages of Online Marketing.

Advantage 1: Ridiculous upside with minimal risks

I started with a few hundred dollars and built an online asset that made me thousands – all while costing me less than $50 in monthly expenses. Online Marketing provides the same income potential as the classic financial freedom vehicles, perhaps even more. Online success stories range from those who earn a few extra hundreds as supplementary income to those mega-deals worth millions of dollars.

By contrast, Online Marketing doesn't come with the same risks and downsides as the classic financial freedom vehicles. It takes minimal resources to start making money online. The costs to keep operating are also low. We can risk and fail a lot, as I did before finding success, and not go broke.

Advantage 2: Work from anywhere

All of my online campaigns and their associated documents fit in a thumb drive that I carry around in my pocket.

I can set up my whole operation by simply plugging my thumb drive into any PC or laptop. I can work from any place that has a working internet connection. There's no need for fancy equipment, a large office, or complicated organizations.

Online Marketing also lets us operate a global business that transcends geographical boundaries and time zones. Those stories that you've heard about an adventurer who built an online store while backpacking through Europe? How about that chill boss who ran his online business on beach offices all over the world? All of those scenarios are possible with Online Marketing.

Advantage 3: Genuine passive income

Most entrepreneurs agree that the most difficult and volatile aspect of running a business is the challenge of the human component. Whether it's leading our employees, working with partners, or dealing with suppliers, the human component opens our business to inconsistencies, errors, conflicts, and even deceit. People also get tired and need to rest.

In Online Marketing, most of our tasks rely on programs, platforms, and systems that don't complain, work ceaselessly, and lend themselves to automatic operation. Automation also allows us to "set it and forget it," thus freeing up a large chunk of our time while still generating income. In effect, we get to build a more stable, peaceful, and reliable passive income vehicle.

That's genuine passive income right there.

Online Marketing and making money online is, without a doubt, a perfect fit for a Millennial's goal of achieving financial freedom.

Passive Income Vehicles and Online Marketing: Wrap-Up and Pro Tips

Employment generates earned income for us but does not lead to financial freedom. This is true no matter how big a salary we get. Passive income is the only key to achieving genuine financial freedom.

There are four classic financial freedom vehicles. However, most of these are difficult to execute for a full-time employee. Online Marketing, a subset among the many ways to make money online, presents a more accessible path to financial freedom.

Through my personal journey to financial freedom, I found Online Marketing to be the best financial freedom vehicle for a full-time, employed Millennial. It requires minimal resources while aligning with the Millennials' predisposition to embrace technology.

Before we proceed to the nuances of the Online Marketing methodology, here are some important reminders and book disclaimers.

Disclaimer 1: Written for the lowest baseline

Appreciate your current standing, and work with what you have now. If you do have access to resources and connections, make the best use of them on your way to financial freedom. Rest assured though, that this book's methodologies cater to the lowest baseline possible – since that was where I began.

I was a fresh graduate Millennial stuck in a nine-to-five job. I started with very little extra money, no knowhow of Online Marketing, no insider friends in the industry, no inheritance or old money from my ancestors, and no existing business empire passed down from my parents. "No silver spoon, no pedigree, and no early mentors," as Starbucks' Howard Schultz put it.

Disclaimer 2: Work around fulltime employment

We know that "rock-bottom to follow a dream" and "leap of faith" success stories are inspiring. We also know that not everyone is willing to go through those states of uncertainty and want. Still, everyone deserves a shot at financial freedom, even without the "go big or go home" attitude to pursue it. The methodology in this book is workable alongside a full-time job and growable until we feel comfortable enough in our online passive income side hustle to quit our day jobs.

Disclaimer 3: Build from absolute zero

When others use the term "from scratch," they simply mean starting a newly created website. The claims omit existing footholds in the industry or insider friends that gave those "newly created" websites a huge jumpstart. Here, when we talk about "from scratch," we mean "absolute zero."

We create our online presence <u>from scratch</u>, gain our industry credentials <u>from scratch</u>, attract our visitors and audience <u>from scratch</u>, and build relationships with industry influencers <u>from scratch</u>. The methodologies here work on a barren soil of no existing assets, no existing clout, no existing followers, no existing connections, and no existing fame or influence.

Disclaimer 4: Effective over groundbreaking

Our focus is on effectiveness. Methods are not included for the sake of sounding cool or showing off strategies that are groundbreaking in theory.

Some of the methods in this book are an amalgamation of the techniques that worked for other Online Marketers whom I trust and respect. These strategies worked for me, but I would not claim that they originated solely from my mind. Credit is given where credit is due.

Disclaimer 5: Practical, modular, and scalable methods

The skills shared in this book are modular. Each step works in synergy with the others to achieve our financial freedom purpose. The skills can also be applied individually, separate from the rest, to existing endeavors. For example, you can apply the traffic generation methods on your existing business separately from the monetization strategies we discuss.

The strategies are also scalable. They are not reliant on hacks, exploits, or fads. Nor are these methods effective only by taking advantage of a window of opportunity. Rather, the methods I share stand on a foundation of timeless principles. They achieve the intended results, even if we use them repeatedly and outside of opportunistic conditions. While the tools may change, the essence of the method will last.

Disclaimer 6: Strategy for a specific goal

Some methods may sound counterintuitive, while others may run contrary to popular tips and techniques. Understand that many practices from mainstream sources apply to enterprise scales or existing brands, not to personal financial goals or campaigns starting from scratch.

Keep in mind that we have a specific aim here – to get us from employed Millennial to financially free in the most efficient and effective way possible.

Consider also that the methods I set before you will take time. These are not get rich quick exploits. Working hard and learning new skills are requirements. Not having much in the way of resources to work with, we can only rely on our grit to start. Let's be mentally prepared to grind now to harvest **money**, **time**, and **choice freedom** later.

The idea is to go beyond delayed gratification and undergo a financial transformation. 'Sacrifice now, enjoy later' is not enough. 'Sacrifice now, better life later' is the goal.

Disclaimer 7: This is a "how-to" reference book

The first read-through shows you the big picture of building passive income online. The aim is to understand each component's purpose, as well as how they synergize to achieve our goal of financial freedom. The second reading, and subsequent reviews, is for putting the methods into practice.

When I was young, my father instilled in me the value of knowledge and skills. He told me that others could steal my money and possessions, but nobody can take away my knowledge and skills. I'm sharing that piece of timeless wisdom with you.

With this book, we'll gain knowledge that can be used to make ourselves financially free. These are marketing principles that we will carry for the rest of our lives.

The power of an enormous business empire now fits in the palms of our hands, encapsulated inside a thumb drive.

Are you ready to do some #adulting and take responsibility for your financial future?

Let's begin.

Chapter 3
Choose the Battlefield

Niche Selection and Intel

"By being everything to everyone, you're nothing to anyone." – Stephen Herfst

Clear with Us. Clear to Them.

A few years back, I participated in a *for toddlers and kids* bazaar with some college friends. Naïve as we were in the realm of business back then, we made many newbie mistakes. The biggest mistake we made, without a doubt, is thinking that it would be smart to sell a wider variety of products – well beyond the theme of the bazaar. After all, toddlers and kids don't go to bazaars alone, right? Grownups are there to accompany them.

Our simple logic was the more products we peddle, the wider base we can cover, and the bigger potential sales. Our smarty-pants wits told us we could monopolize the grownups market while our competitors are fighting over the toddlers and kids. Brilliant strategy, right? Not quite.

First, we were surprised nobody ratted us out to the organizers or got us removed from the event for not following the theme.

The bigger surprise was that instead of attracting every possible buyer, our strategy was repelling potential customers. Our booth was unable to project a unified theme, and that confused the shoppers who were there to buy kiddie stuff. Majority of the people took a passing glance at our booth and moved on. I felt the truth in the saying – "a confused mind always says NO."

We lost a chunk of money in that bazaar. I did learn the importance of defining my business and understanding the landscape where I am operating. If we are clear with our business, then our business will be clear to our customers. That's where **niche selection and intel** come in.

Choose Your Niche Topic Area

The first step in any Online Marketing endeavor is to choose our niche topic area.

A **niche** is a small segment of a general market or industry. Niche may also refer to a sub-topic of a broad subject.

The idea of serving a niche is to identify a specialized group of people with shared needs, wants, and requirements – as opposed to trying to appeal to everyone. It's costly – and impossible – to cater to everyone.

Marketing to a niche, instead of a general market, allows us to focus limited resources on gaining maximum impact. Reaching a small segment of the population is cheaper. Tailor-fit marketing messages lead to better responses. Overall, starting a niche market gives us greater chances of succeeding at making money online.

Step 1: Brainstorm niche topic ideas

The process of choosing a niche topic starts with a brainstorming exercise. We want to come up with a list of niche ideas that we can pursue.

It may be hard to pull ideas for niche topics out of thin air, so here are two resources we can use to kick-start our brainstorming process. We can use either one or both, to suit our needs.

Let's try to come up with a list of **at least 50 possible niche topics**.

Resource 1: *EzineArticles* category list

EzineArticles is an article directory where independent authors submit articles on every topic under the sun. The

EzineArticles category listing represents all major topic categories with a substantial number of articles submitted by users. These are major topics of discussion and are rich niches to get into.

1. Go to http://www.ezinearticles.com/category-guidelines.html.
2. Scan through the deep subjects (i.e., subtopics) and list the niche topics that resonate with you.

Resource 2: *For Dummies* store catalog

For Dummies is a popular brand of how-to books covering a very wide range of topics. Book brands or series like the ***For Dummies*** library undergo extensive market research before coming out with books on any topic. They need to turn a profit, after all. In that case, we can surmise that a particular niche topic is viable if there's a ***For Dummies*** book written on the subject.

1. Go to http://www.dummies.com/store/All-Titles.html.
2. Click through a major topic that resonates with you from the list on the left.
3. Dig deeper by clicking on a sub topic that you like from the expanded list.
4. Choose to sort by *Publication Date*. Recent books make better niche topic candidates.
5. List the book titles that resonate with you. Remove the ***For Dummies*** from the title to derive your niche topic.

<u>Notes for this section</u>

- Don't hesitate. If it resonates, include it in your list. Lean on the side of inclusion. Gather what ideas you can first.
- Don't look too far ahead. You might feel that you're not an expert on a particular topic. You might have no idea about what products or services to sell in a niche. Don't worry. We address those concerns later. For now, list the topics that you feel like considering.

- Add niche topic ideas that come naturally to you, regardless of whether they appear among the resources above or not. Here is a list of guide questions (I got the idea for this from Danny Iny of <u>Mirasee.com</u>) that can help you expand your niche topic ideas.

  - o What are you interested in?
  - o What would you want to do with your time, even if no one paid you to do it?
  - o What do you see that's messed up in people's lives that you can help fix?
  - o Imagine this scenario – you've won a contest, and your prize is you get to spend an entire year studying <u>any one thing</u> you want. The only catch is that once you begin your year, you can't bail out in the middle, or change topics.
  - o What do you enjoy doing? Examine your social media pictures and activities calendar for the past month and use that as your basis for answering the question.

- It's better to overpopulate your list. It's easy to remove the items that don't feel right later rather than to have a selection of niche topics that is too small.

Step 2: Validate your best niche topics

Now that we have a long list, it's time to shorten that list. We create a shortlist of the most viable niche topics through a validation process. Run each niche topic idea through several validation filters to help separate the promising niches from the bleak ones. We'll then build our Online Marketing business around the winning niche topic.

Just like a water-filtration system, the good stuff goes through while the bad elements fall off at each stage of the filtration process. In our case, bad niche ideas get removed, and the good niches move further through the filters. In the end, we'll have a more manageable list from which to choose a winning topic.

Filter 1: Affinity filter

Affinity refers to niche topics to which we have a natural inclination. Affinity with a niche topic gives us an advantage because we can provide immediate value to the industry. For each niche topic idea on our list, we'll retain those that pass the **affinity filter** and cross off the ones that don't. We have an affinity with the topic if we can answer YES to <u>any one</u> of these guide questions.

- Are you familiar with this topic? Have you read books, watched videos, attended seminars, or followed experts on this subject?
- Do other people perceive you as an expert on this topic? Do your friends ask you for advice, information, or help on this subject?
- Do you have an existing foothold in the industry? Do you have exclusive access to a group of people with similar needs and wants about this topic? Do you have an existing audience for this subject?

Filter 2: Market filter

Now we have a trimmed down list of niche topic ideas that passed through the affinity filter. We will then subject this trimmed down list to the **market filter**. The market filter is about determining if the niche topic has profit potential.

This simple test allows us to guesstimate if we can make money on this topic. We are here to work for financial freedom, after all.

1. Go to <u>https://www.amazon.com/</u>.
2. Type in the niche topic in the search box located at the top of the webpage.
3. Sift through the results and take note of products that have reviews.

4. If you can find at least <u>five different products</u> with a minimum of <u>50 reviews each</u>, it means there are people spending on this niche topic, so it passes the market filter. Otherwise, cross that topic off the list.

5. Do this for all remaining niche topic ideas.

Filter 3: Tie-breaker filters

We have further reduced the number of possible niche topics you can pursue using the market filter.

Now we are confident that we can provide value and be rewarded for these niche topics. This makes each of the surviving niche topics viable for Online Marketing. We have a great shot at financial freedom pursuing any of these niches.

We can further refine the remaining niche topic ideas by passing them through **tie-breaker filters**. These filters are optional, though they can help us find the best topic to pursue. We can trim this list further by asking if these niches are part of the **big three** and if they have room for **easy differentiation**. Niches that get the answer of YES <u>to both</u> of these questions break the tie, and they are perfect candidates for Online Marketing.

- **Tiebreaker 1: Big three?** Does this topic deal with matters concerning health, wealth, or love? These **big three industries** are proven moneymakers through history. Health deals with physical and mental health, as well as vanity and grooming. Wealth covers topics on making money and increasing net worth. Love discusses things like dating, relationships, marriage, and family.

- **Tiebreaker 2: Easy differentiation?** Extending from the *Amazon* search I used as an example, are there at least five different <u>books</u> BY DIFFERENT AUTHORS on the niche topic? The presence of multiple books and authors signals a rich niche topic area that allows for a wide range of discussions. These niches are hard to saturate because the diversity of the topic grants room for easy differentiation among experts within the niche. Weight loss for women, for example, is a niche topic that has room for many experts to tackle from multiple different angles and unique perspectives. Various viewpoints on exercise, diet, motivation, supplements, equipment, biochemistry, even surgical procedures exist to cross-examine this one niche topic. Easy differentiation indicates that you can fit in the industry and provide a unique offering.

Notes for this section

- Search algorithms aren't perfect. Always use your best judgment when analyzing search results. Determine which results are relevant and disregard invalid items.
- When analyzing reviews for niche topic validation purposes, it doesn't matter if the reviews are positive or negative. An industry with lots of negative reviews for its products offers us an opportunity. You can profit by entering the niche and providing a better product or service.

Step 3: Select the winning niche

Now that leaves us with a very select list of niche topics to consider – niche topics we have the strongest chances of succeeding. We can provide value using these topics. They all have profit potential. They can support another player (you) entering the industry with ease.

From this shortlist, choose one you want to pursue. We will then build our Online Marketing business around this niche topic.

Keep your niche shortlist for future reference. While we've chosen our winning niche, we are not married to it. Should the results of our efforts perform below our expectations, we can always pivot, revisit the list, and pursue another niche.

Great job! Now we have a niche topic for our Online Marketing. We have just chosen the battlefield to fight for our financial freedom.

Gathering Niche Intel

Now that we've narrowed the field down to one niche topic, it's time to gather intelligence – **intel** – on that niche. Gaining valuable information before creating or launching Online Marketing campaigns helps us make intelligent decisions from the beginning. This gives us the highest chances of success, especially if this is our first try with a new niche.

The main idea of gathering intel is so that we never fly blindly into our chosen niche.

When it comes to niche intelligence, we would need to research three key pieces of intel on our niche – **niche keywords**, **niche influencers**, and **niche crowd**.

Intel 1: Niche keywords

Every niche topic contains **keywords**. For our research purposes, keywords are words or phrases that form the terms, jargon, lingo, synonyms, and even subtopics relevant to a subject.

Niche keywords form the vocabulary that the population of that niche uses to communicate about the subject. Being familiar with the vocabulary of the niche then allows us to use the proper terminologies for our Online Marketing efforts.

1. Go to http://www.soovle.com/.
2. Type your niche topic into the search box in the middle of the webpage.
3. The results will show the relevant niche keywords derived from different sources. Take note of the relevant keywords from the results.
4. You can also go to https://www.keywordtool.io/ and perform a more extensive niche keyword search using their keyword research tool.

<u>Notes for this section</u>

- As with other algorithms, these keyword research tools are not perfect. Use your judgment to pick out the keywords that are relevant to you and your chosen niche.
- By entering your main niche topic, you'll get a set of niche keywords. You can use those niche keywords results on the same keyword research tools (i.e., ***Soovle.com*** or ***Keywordtool.io***) to help you identify more relevant and related niche keywords.
- While some of these tools offer paid versions and services, the free versions are enough for your purposes.
- This exercise is only meant to give us a serviceable vocabulary of the jargon of our chosen niche, so don't overdo it. You may end up doing research forever. The basic terms used by the niche population are enough.

Intel 2: Niche influencers

Chances are, we are not the first to open up our chosen niche topic area. There are already known and established personalities operating in any given niche. They are considered "influencers."

These influencers serve as major forces – shaping the thoughts and opinions of their niche, including businesses, consumers, and other influencers.

Identifying and following niche influencers enable us to remain updated on the trends of our niche. Also, influencers are reliable sources for benchmarking of techniques that are working well in a niche. Whether we are brainstorming for a blog post or contemplating the prices for our products in the future, these influencers provide valuable benchmarks we can use as starting points for decision-making.

Step 1: Identify niche influencers and their respective primary website

In the digital age, it's quite easy to identify the influencers of our niche. They have prominent online presences – usually they own websites that receive regular visits from their big audience. They also have official accounts (on social media or elsewhere) with substantial followings. If we are entering a new niche and are unfamiliar with the niche influencers, these tools can help.

- **Tool 1: Buzzsumo influencers tool.** *Buzzsumo* is one of the most comprehensive content marketing tools available online. Its powerful functionalities monitor and analyze the most viral posts and most influential experts, among other things. Keep *Buzzsumo* close, because we'll use this tool for other purposes in the future.

    1. Visit https://app.buzzsumo.com/.
    2. Click on the *Influencers* tab at the top.
    3. Type your niche topic or a **niche keyword** into the search bar at the top.
    4. List down the name of the influencers. Take note of their website addresses.

- **Tool 2: Amazon book authors.** *Amazon* is the biggest e-commerce website on the planet, with billions of business transactions and customer interactions per year. It also serves as a goldmine of valuable marketing data. Book authors, especially those who have publishers or who have achieved best-seller status, are definitely influencers in their fields with substantial fan bases.

    1. Visit https://www.amazon.com/.
    2. Type your niche topic or a niche keyword in the search bar at the top.
    3. Examine the search results, and scan for well-performing books and list their authors' names.
    4. Click on the author name to visit the author's *Amazon* **profile**, copy the link to the author's blog or main website if listed.

5. If the website in not listed on the author's **Amazon** profile, you can do a search using https://www .google.com/ by typing the author's name into the search field to find their primary website. Add the niche topic to the search phrase if authors and people of the same name appear in the search results (i.e., "Kurt Roswell Online Marketing").

Step 2: Determine the influencer website's estimated monthly traffic volume

Now that we have a list of niche influencer names and the corresponding website addresses, it's time to determine how influential they are. A simple way to guesstimate this is to see how many visitors their primary websites receive per month.

1. Go to https://www.similarweb.com/.
2. Enter the influencer's website address in the search bar on the upper left of the screen. Search suggestions may appear for popular websites.
3. Scroll down the *Traffic Overview* section and copy the number of *Total Visits* alongside the corresponding website.
4. Use the traffic numbers to sort through your list of influencers from largest to lowest. This will give you an idea of the biggest names in your niche.

Notes for this section

- Influencers that are companies or brands usually have a prominent figure behind them. It's more advisable to follow the person, but following a brand will also yield valuable insights.
- Books with multiple reviews and purchases represent an influential author. Keep this in mind when researching influencers from https://www.amazon.com/.
- We only need to follow the biggest influencers in our niche, since they represent the major clout in the industry we've chosen.

Intel 3: Niche crowd

Our **niche population** is comprised of different categories of participants overall – from businesses and influencers all the way to consumers. From that niche population, the **niche crowd** represents the group of people that can potentially become our customers.

The niche crowd forms the economic base of the niche. They buy products and services as solutions to their needs and wants. We enter a niche with the aim of serving the niche crowd. It is in satisfying the niche crowd's problems, issues, and concerns that leads to financial rewards down the line.

Knowing our niche crowd gives us a strong foundation for great marketing. With a clear picture of our niche crowd's background, needs, and wants, we can echo their problems to them and provide the best solutions. Doing so will increase the likelihood that they'll respond favorably to our messages and offers.

To gain a deep understanding of our niche crowd, we need to know **who they are** and **what they need and want**.

Step 1: Who they are?

The online world can be an impersonal environment that we forget – human beings are behind those *posts*, *comments*, and *uploads* (the ones that matter, at least). As a marketer, it's important to have a clear mental image of who exactly we are catering to. Having an accurate persona of our niche crowd takes away the guesswork and increases our chances of successfully finding and serving them.

1. Go to https://www.google.com/.
2. Type your niche topic or keyword and append the word **for** into the search bar in the middle. For example, type *weight loss for* and DON'T press the *enter* key. Instead, let ***Google*** show you the suggestions.

3. Each situation is different, so assess the suggestions and look only for relevant niche crowd personas. A search for *best "dog training" for* yielded *best dog training for <u>german shepherds</u>*, *best dog training for <u>aggressive dogs</u>*, and *best dog training for <u>puppies</u>* as relevant suggestion results.
4. Repeat the process for other niche keywords to identify additional niche crowd personas within the niche.

Step 2: What they need and want?

After identifying the personas that compose our niche crowd, it's time to complete the picture and learn about their questions, problems, and concerns.

Knowing the issues that are going through our niche crowd's minds gives us an advantage. Imagine if we could speak clearly about their problems and find the words relatable to our niche crowd. That insight allows us to connect even more deeply with them.

We can derive our niche crowd's questions, problems, and concerns from several sources.

- **Source 1: Niche forum discussions. Forums** have been a staple of the internet since its early years. Forums are simple websites resembling message boards made of different threads and topics. These types of websites facilitate in-depth discussions on a variety of topics among its members.

    1. Go to https://www.google.com/ to search for forums in your niche topic.
    2. Type in your niche topic or keyword and append the word **+forum**. For example, *weight loss <u>+forum</u>*. The + indicates that the word is a must-have component of the search.
    3. Look through the results and visit the relevant quality forums. A quick way to check the quality of a given forum is to see if it has a lot of recent activity. A good forum is one where there are multiple

   threads and comments posted *today* or, at the very least, at a recent date.

4. Visit the threads and copy the posts that are questions or problems. Copy the entire question post verbatim – include the title and details, and keep the grammatical errors and multiple punctuations. You want to keep track of your niche crowd's questions and problems exactly as your market expresses them.
5. Do so for other niche keywords to find more forums.

- **Source 2: Amazon reviews. *Amazon*** is really a gold mine of rich consumer information. That's why we keep going back to it for our research purposes. It's a great place for gathering insights on our niche crowd's psyche.

  1. Visit https://www.amazon.com/.
  2. Type your niche topic or keyword in the search bar at the top.
  3. Examine the search results for products related to your niche.
  4. Read the <u>negative</u> reviews. Click on the *1-star* and *2-star* reviews. You'll get a lot of insights on your niche crowd's concerns.
  5. Take note of the relevant reviews. Those that have clear questions or emotional expressions of concern (i.e., frustration and anger) are great candidates. Copy the entire review verbatim.
  6. Repeat on multiple products and different niche keywords to find more useful reviews.

- **Source 3: Reddit. *Reddit*** started as a social bookmarking website but has since evolved into an active community for discussion about all sorts of topics. The value of ***Reddit*** is in its active, intelligent (most of the time, sarcastic), and "take no BS" user base. Therefore, ***Reddit*** can be a great source of insights regarding your niche crowd's mind.

1. Visit https://www.reddit.com/.
2. Type in your niche topic or keyword in the search bar on the right.
3. The search results come in two forms – **subreddits** above and **posts** below. Think of subreddits as threads that contain many posts on a topic. Posts, on the other hand, link directly to the individual post page. Focus on the subreddits to see multiple posts organized into their respective topics.
4. Click through the results and check out the posts of users.
5. Similar to the other resources above, look for questions and problems. Copy the title and details or comments verbatim.

<u>Notes for this section</u>

- Don't go crazy with research. At this point, we only need a general idea of the niche. Having a general idea is better than having no clue, after all. **Three to five** identifiable niche crowd personas are enough to start. **20 to 30** pieces of quality problems, questions, and concerns for our niche crowd can also get us going.
- The richness and emotional intensity of the niche crowd's posts are important. The length of the post is a good eye test to indicate the richness of a comment or review. Exclamation points, on the other hand, are good indicators of emotional intensity. Only serious questions, problems, and concerns are long, well thought out, and fueled by emotion – these present great opportunities to provide value.

Niche Selection and Intel: Wrap-Up and Pro Tips

The first step in any business – especially Online Marketing – is to define our boundaries. The exercises in this chapter allow us to choose a viable niche topic to tackle, get familiar with the lingo and subtopics of that niche, identify the thought leaders of our niche, and gain in-depth knowledge of the niche crowd we aim to serve.

Our output by the end of this chapter includes deciding on a niche topic and producing the three niche intel documents – **niche keywords**, **niche influencers**, and **niche crowd**. This preliminary research will help us make informed business decisions.

Here are some additional best practices to keep in mind.

Tip 1: Be a big fish in a small pond

Working on a smaller, more defined niche allows us to focus our resources while we gain a foothold in the industry. Once we've made a name for ourselves, we can then expand our topic area more effectively. We'll have better chances of reaching "big fish" status starting in a small pond than trying to conquer the big ocean from the onset.

Tip 2: Keep updating the niche intel documents

The niche intel documents are dynamic tools that you can use as a reference for future decisions. It's a good idea to keep adding to them if – and only if – we have the time to do so. We update the niche keywords document as we encounter more jargon and sub-topics. We do the same for the niche influencer documents for experts we meet as we grow into the industry. We add to the niche crowd document as we gain a better understanding of our target market.

Tip 3: Not a lifetime marriage

Choosing a niche topic at this stage is not set in stone. We are not bound to this niche topic for life. We can always return and pivot and enter another related niche, or completely move to a different topic area.

The idea is to go out quickly and see how the market responds, then make further decisions from that point. Don't be afraid to go out, fail, then try again. That's the life of an entrepreneur.

Experiencing the first breeze of success will make all the failures worth it. This I can promise you.

Deciding on a niche sets our online endeavor on a defined course. Gathering niche intel guarantees that we don't trek that course blind.

With an informed plan of approach in hand, it's time to start building on the foundations of our online business.

Chapter 4

A Superior Approach to Building Online Businesses

Agile Online Income Machine

"Everyone has a story to tell or product to sell. Know your audience before you open your mouth." – Anonymous

Beating the Business Odds

A countdown runs in my head as my finger nervously hovers over the *launch* button. In a few seconds, I will finally put my work out there for the world to see. This is the culmination of months of tireless work and sleepless nights negotiating with vendors, assembling the pieces, testing the process, and tweaking the output.

It's ready now. I muster up all the courage, feel the curve of the mouse under my hands, apply enough pressure, and finally click the button. The business engine starts running and my online business gets going. We are live.

Then all I hear are crickets – maybe a smidgen of tumbleweed in the breeze. As it turns out, nobody cares for what I've created.

Most people make the mistake of making business decisions based on intuition and personal preferences, especially those who are embarking on an enterprising endeavor for the first time – be it starting a business, publishing a blog, starting a video channel, launching an e-commerce website, or creating a product.

These aspiring entrepreneurs spend substantial amounts of resources building <u>their</u> product, service, article, video, or website only to end up launching output that they love, but nobody else wants. It's no wonder that, according to a **Fortune** article, nine out of 10 startups fail – with *No Market Need* being the top reason for failure (*Run Out of Cash* comes in second).

Having failed multiple times before figuring out what works, I endured the brunt of the cost, fatigue, and frustration of launching full-scale online businesses only to be met with apathy. Those painful experiences forced me to change my perspective and to approach Online Marketing with several key differences.

First, I followed the idea of the *Minimum Viable Product (MVP)* popularized by Eric Ries in his best-selling book **The Lean Startup**.

Instead of launching a full-scale online business, I settle for the minimum viable campaign that I can launch quickly if only to build an audience and start gathering feedback right away. This way, I don't spend a lot of resources before the launch. I also gain enough wiggle room to develop my business at a steady, manageable pace.

Second, I realized that I kept failing because I was making subjective business decisions that weren't grounded in what was happening in the market I sought to enter.

Instead of relying on personal biases, I've decided to make informed actions based on my audience's sentiments. The effect is that I don't build my online businesses blindly. This also gives me confidence that my output will get a positive response.

Last, I accepted the fact that the modern world is ever-changing – and that it's changing rapidly.

Instead of following rigid methods and techniques, I emphasize business flexibility and the ability to adapt to sudden changes. This approach allows me to future-proof my online businesses while minimizing the negative impact of disruptive developments.

All these principles paved way to a unique approach for making money online – a method that needs no more than $50 of overhead a month and 3 hours of productive work a week. This proves to be the most favorable approach for Millennials, who are most likely starting from scratch. Let me introduce the **Agile Online Income Machine.**

Agile Online Income Machine Overview

The main principle of the Agile Online Income Machine is to capture an audience pool first by collecting qualified email addresses.

In the online world, a captive audience can be represented by *page likes*, *channel subscribers*, *account followers*, and everything in between. For our Online Marketing and financial freedom purposes, the concrete representative of our captive audience is a database of email addresses.

After collecting qualified email addresses, we then develop our online business along the responses of our audience base. See the illustration of the Agile Online Income Machine below.

Our focus as the Online Marketer is to identify and attract our niche crowd. We must nurture them into **buyers**. Once they become buyers, we will make money and realize financial freedom. Along the way, our Agile Online Income Machine systematically cultivates our niche crowd, stage by stage.

The system itself resembles a **funnel** covering three stages – **Stage 1: Audience-building machine, Stage 2: Relationship-building machine**, and **Stage 3: Passive income machine**. We then use different **traffic generation** methods to attract our target market through these different stages. The niche crowd goes through the system as **visitors**, turns into our **audience**, then into **fans**, and, finally, into **buyers**. These mechanisms are the focus for the rest of this book.

Diving deeper into the process, we start by putting up traffic sources to attract people from our niche crowd to visit a distinct website we've set up. On our website, the visitors opt to download a **lead magnet** by signing up and subscribing to our mailing list.

Inside our mailing list, we continue the conversation as our audience engages our **sequence emails** that we have running along a **nurture email series**. We then weave relevant **affiliate product** messages, or our product messages, into our nurture email series to entice fans to buy what we offer.

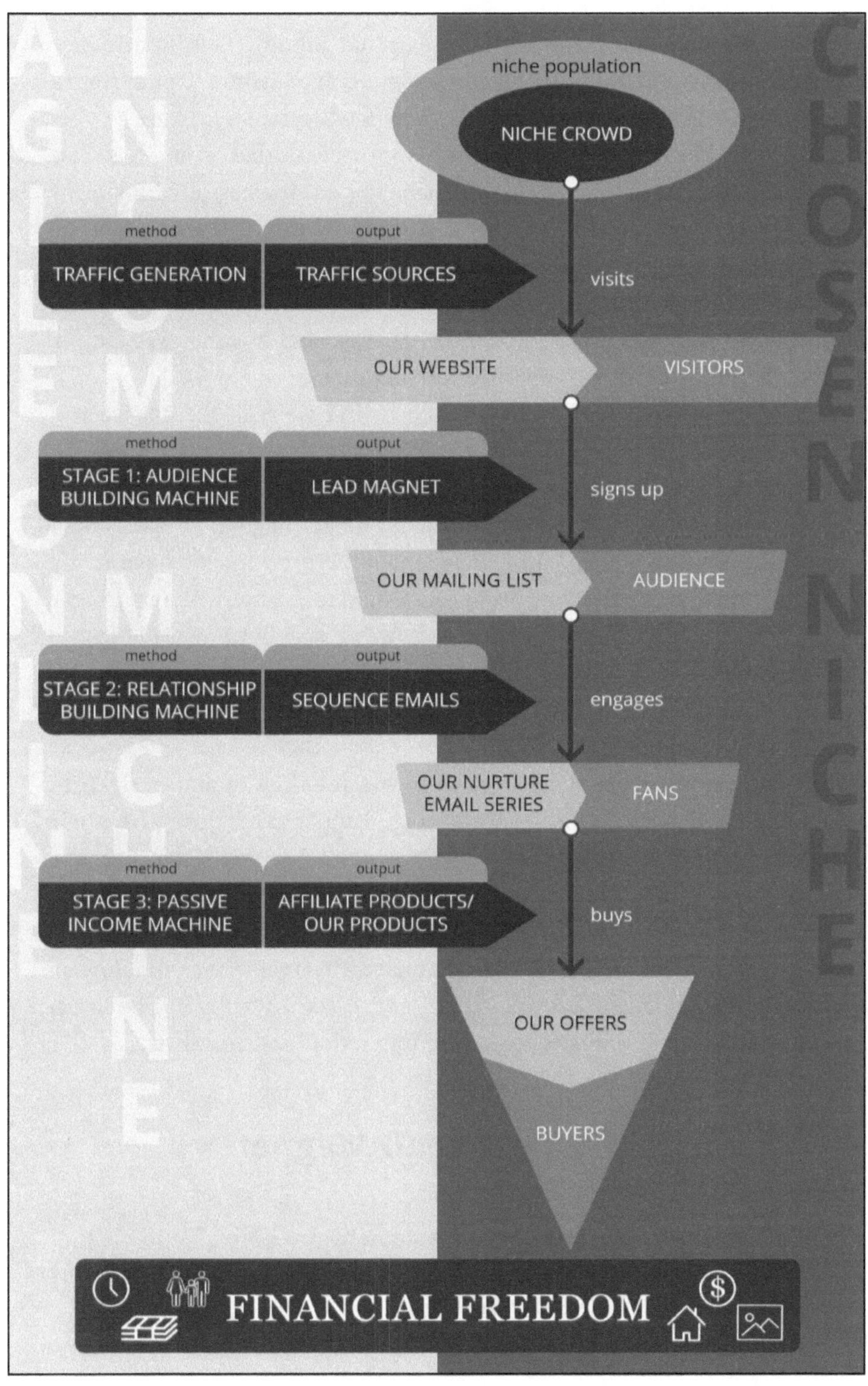
niche population
NICHE CROWD
visits
method
TRAFFIC GENERATION
output
TRAFFIC SOURCES
OUR WEBSITE
VISITORS
method
STAGE 1: AUDIENCE BUILDING MACHINE
output
LEAD MAGNET
signs up
OUR MAILING LIST
AUDIENCE
method
STAGE 2: RELATIONSHIP BUILDING MACHINE
output
SEQUENCE EMAILS
engages
OUR NURTURE EMAIL SERIES
FANS
method
STAGE 3: PASSIVE INCOME MACHINE
output
AFFILIATE PRODUCTS/ OUR PRODUCTS
buys
OUR OFFERS
BUYERS
FINANCIAL FREEDOM

Our precious buyers finally earn us money. Our multi-stage machine ensures that money comes as passive income. Our system's consistent growth leads to a financially free lifestyle.

The key characteristic of our approach is that every business decision we take is based on our niche crowd. We began with a clear understanding of our niche crowd via our niche crowd research.

Now, we rely on our niche crowd to determine the websites we create, the content we publish, and the offers we present. The principle is to let our target market express what it wants. We simply provide it for them at every stage of the process.

The advantage of this approach is that we take the guesswork, luck, and our personal biases out of the business equation. We no longer have to speculate about which words and phrases will move our target market to take action. We no longer have to guesstimate a website and pray for visitor engagement. We no longer have to fly blind on what product our prospects would love to buy. We no longer have to waste valuable resources throwing spaghetti at walls to see what sticks.

Of course, the illustration above is an oversimplification – broad strokes, if you will.

In reality, each stage in the process requires the more delicate science and art of Online Marketing. People don't just give their email addresses away freely – and you can't just take them because that's spamming. Nor do people buy offers simply because they get an email.

As such, let me share with you an essential tool that will allow us to capture our niche crowd's email addresses lawfully and open up the line for further relationship building – the **lead magnet**.

The Best Lead Magnet

Lead magnets are free, yet valuable, incentives we give to visitors in exchange for their contact information. They are also known as **freemiums, lead baits, opt-in incentives,** or **ethical bribes**.

The lead magnet can be as simple as a short report or a free version of a product, or as complex as a 30-minute free consultation or a free webinar. The key trait here is <u>valuable</u>.

Simply because we offer this incentive for free doesn't automatically make it valuable to our visitors. Free junk is still junk, and junk won't entice our visitors to share their email addresses with us.

Keep in mind, never deceive visitors into giving up their email addresses. That means no hyping up lead magnet benefits, no bait-and-switch actions, no adding email addresses without permission. These misleading practices start the business relationship off on the wrong foot. In the end, it will be impossible to gain our audience's trust in any way – much less get them to buy products from us.

Now, assuming the lowest possible baseline of novices starting from scratch, the best lead magnet to develop is one that is easy to create while offering tremendous perceived value. A lead magnet in **eReport** form and discusses powerful **niche tools** exactly fits this bill.

An **eReport** is a short report in PDF document format that our visitors can download. It's easy to produce using common word processing and PDF converter tools. More importantly, eReports scale easily – allowing unlimited downloads in exchange for email addresses of visitors without incurring any additional costs.

Regarding content, **niche tools** work great as a lead magnet. Sharing the essential <u>tools</u> that solve the most common problems and issues encountered within your niche works better than teaching your visitors a skill or method to achieve the same. After all, it's more enjoyable to buy or use a tool than it is to spend time learning a skill.

As a start, get to know your niche crowd's struggles. You can refer to the niche crowd research we did from an earlier chapter. Analyze and determine the most prominent problems, issues, concerns, and complaints that your niche crowd is experiencing. From there, search and list **five** tools that can solve these prominent problems, issues, concerns, and complaints.

"Tools," in this context, is a very loose term. It goes beyond a physical tool or appliance. Tools can be software, an online program, an Excel file, a quick life hack, or even a simple productivity technique. The key difference of skills versus tools is that skills need time and discipline to learn, while tools are ready to use immediately.

Producing Our Lead Magnet: Going Fast and Effective

After coming up with **five** tools that could help our niche crowd, it's time to produce the lead magnet that our visitors can download.

Step 1: Outline

The process for creating content starts with an **outline**. Regardless of whether the output is an article, an audio, a video, or even software, we need some semblance of an overview to see how the different parts of our lead magnet connect and flow logically. An outline allows us to produce output that "makes sense" from the perspective of the reader or consumer.

If you already know how to go about writing and publishing the report for the niche tools you've listed, go ahead and follow your process. Here's an outline for a niche tool lead magnet that has proven to be effective and simple to follow – *benefit hook ➜ what is the tool? ➜ how to use the tool to achieve the benefit? ➜ additional pro tips.*

Element 1: Benefit hook

I always like to start describing a tool with a benefit hook. This involves describing, in vivid detail, the benefits or results that the reader can enjoy or achieve, without revealing the tool first.

It goes along the lines of "imagine if you could [achieved results]" or "picture this, you [wonderful benefits]" or "what if you can [valuable outcomes]" and you go on painting a clear picture of the positive outcome that can happen once they use this particular tool.

Starting with the benefit hook grabs the attention and raises the interest of your readers. This motivates, subconsciously entices even, your readers to keep on reading.

Element 2: What is the tool?

After we've hooked our readers with our intro, we can reveal the tool. Show what the tool is and lay out its basic features.

Element 3: How to use the tool to achieve the benefit?

Once we've revealed the tool, we can describe, step by step, how we use the tool to solve their problem and achieve the desired result.

Describe the procedure in detail and present it in bullet points or numbered lists. We need to assume that this is the first time our reader is using this tool, so don't leave any details out. We close this part by reiterating the attainable results of following this procedure and using this tool.

Element 4: Additional pro tips

We cap the section off by providing additional pro tips, or best practices, to enhance the usage of this tool. Enumerate reminders too, so that the reader can use the tool correctly. We can also share some tips for the optimal use of the tool.

Follow this outline for each of the tools included in the lead magnet. This outline will enable us to finish writing our lead magnet in no time.

Step 2: Enhance and polish

Once we've put all the text down, we can add supporting images and screenshots to enhance our lead magnet. Images allow our readers to visualize what we're describing better while also serving as visual breaks from all the texts.

Once we've included images, we can add professional polish and credibility to our lead magnet by fixing the layout design and adding a cover page. This allows our lead magnet to be more aesthetically pleasing.

The layout design makes our lead magnet more readable. The cover page wraps our lead magnet up in a beautiful bow.

1. Search the web (i.e., use Google - https://www.google.com/) for layout and cover design inspiration.
2. Use your word processor's basic formatting features to fix the layout design of the lead magnet.
3. Go to https://www.canva.com/ to create the cover design. **Canva** is a free and easy-to-use online graphic design app. You'll be able to create wonderful designs even if you don't have any graphic design experience.
4. Optional, visit https://boxshot.com/3d-pack/3d-book/ to create a 3D rendering of the lead magnet.

Step 3: Convert to PDF

When we are already satisfied with our lead magnet's content, layout, and cover page, we can go on and convert it into a PDF document.

Most word processors have the *convert to PDF* functionality built into them. If yours doesn't, you can go to https://www.smallpdf .com/pdf-converter and convert your document there.

We now have a lead magnet ready to provide value for our niche crowd in exchange for their email addresses.

We already know how valuable our lead magnet is and how it can help our niche crowd deal with their most pressing problems and obstacles. However, our visitors don't know that yet.

We need to convey the value of our lead magnet enticingly to move our niche crowd to action (i.e., download our lead magnet) without hesitation.

Lead Magnet Benefit Statement

The **lead magnet benefit statement** is a short enticing description of our lead magnet. Think of this as our lead magnet's "elevator pitch." It underlines our lead magnet's identity and purpose. If we only have a fraction of a second to explain and captivate our visitors with our lead magnet, how would we phrase it?

Our lead magnet benefit statement needs to be short – internet users have short attention spans. We need to value that short attention like it is water in a desert.

Brevity is king because the spots online where we intend to use our lead magnet benefit statement come with character limits. We need to convey our valuable lead magnet message using limited digital real estate.

Besides being short, lead magnet benefit statements need to be expressed in terms of **features** and **benefits**, rather than features alone. The difference between features and benefits is a critical distinction to understand so that we can effectively communicate to our target market online.

Features vs. Benefits

Features refer to characteristics of an offering – a product, service, or lead magnet. These are the defining traits and attributes of what a product has, or is.

We refer to features when we talk about the composition of the product (what it is made of), what the product does, and the product's offer terms (price, guarantees, delivery).

Benefits refer to outcomes and results that users will accomplish or enjoy by using the product, service, or lead magnet. Benefits talk about life after solving the problem, overcoming the obstacle, or working out the issues.

One of the most famous, and often used, illustration of features vs. benefits is Steve Jobs' presentation of the classic 1st generation iPod in 2001.

Instead of saying that the device has 5GB of storage capacity (a feature), Steve Jobs sold the iPod with this great benefit statement – "1,000 songs in your pocket."

To make the concept more concrete, here are some examples of contrasting features vs. benefits.

FEATURES	**BENEFITS**
Instant access	Enjoy immediately after purchase
Portable	Bring with you wherever you go
Four-wheel drive	Travel over any terrain
Personalized customer service	Receive one-on-one attention
Integrated email	Check your emails anywhere

Features are superficial. They can only scratch the surface of a reader's motivations. They can work on enthusiasts and the technically-inclined but will fly over the heads of an interested prospect. Features alone can't move readers to action.

Benefits work better because they trigger the mental, as well as the emotional, faculties of the reader. An emotional push is exactly what gets people to move.

To craft a powerful lead magnet benefit statement

A simple formula to craft a powerful benefit statement for our lead magnet is **1/3 feature + 2/3 benefit**.

For a benefit statement to be effective, it needs to use both features and benefits, but favor the benefits. Here are some examples of lead magnet benefit statements.

- *Free report lets you discover the EXACT tools the pros are using to launch profitable campaigns EACH TIME.*
- *Want random people on the internet to buy stuff from you? If so, you need an email list. This free report will show you how to get your first 100 email subscribers.*
- *This report gives you the secrets to getting the right type of traffic to your site, plus what to do with all that traffic.*

From these examples, the phrases *free report* or *report* are features while the rest of the statement is dedicated to benefits.

Now it's your turn to create the benefit statement for your lead magnet.

Agile Online Income Machine: Wrap-Up and Pro Tips

There are many ways to make money online. We now understand that <u>not all</u> of them are accessible to full-time employees. Even fewer are methods that generate passive income which can lead to financial freedom. The Agile Online Income Machine methodology is one such method. The method's modular approach aims to maximize our upside while minimizing risk. It also offers our business the flexibility to adapt to unpredictable conditions after launching.

The Agile Online Income Machine starts with creating a lead magnet as an ethical bribe for visitors in exchange for their email addresses. Going through the steps laid out in this chapter allows us to produce a highly valued lead magnet quickly, and at the least possible cost.

Aside from the output of a lead magnet, here are some unique perspectives and tips regarding the Agile Online Income Machine.

Tip 1: Audience as the main basis

The truth is this – nobody cares what we know or what we like. That makes our intuition a weak basis from which to start making business decisions. People who spend and buy only care for what we, our products, or our services can do for them.

Instead of starting our business by writing our first article, producing our first video, or stocking inventory for our products like most aspiring entrepreneurs do, we start by developing our audience. Amassing a substantial audience base and using them as the basis for decisions is a more reliable approach to building a business.

Tip 2: Email is valuable and stable

While chat rooms, forum websites, social media platforms, messaging programs, voice chat software, and video conference apps have come, evolved, peaked, and gone, email stayed the same. No single entity controls the email protocol. That is why it doesn't change form, nor is it capable of screwing our business with sudden policy changes.

We can also expect every online user to have an email address. After all, email addresses are necessary to sign up for accounts on websites, services, and apps. People also treat their email addresses the way they treat their phone numbers – with care and discernment.

Email correspondences are also innately warmer and more purposeful than conversations over public social media networks and message boards.

In that sense, email continues to be the most reliable medium of engagement with our audience online.

Tip 3: Audience as our most important asset

We can find more success in offering decent products to a captive audience than peddling amazing products to a cold crowd.

On top of that, nurturing an audience gives us a lucrative avenue for repeat customers. Having a captive audience also provides a testing ground for future campaigns and product launches.

Our audience is our most important business asset. Let's treat them as they should be treated – with care and an eye on their value to our business.

Tip 4: A sizable audience opens opportunities

Having a sizable audience opens up many opportunities. It makes business easier and easier to do as we grow our audience.

This is how athletes become endorsers for products outside of their sport. This is how celebrities get paid millions to tweet product recommendations. They all have sizable audiences who follow or idolize them.

In our online business, commanding a sizable audience can get us exclusive deals not available to the public. It's also easy to partner with industry influencers when you can show your audience size. It's also fairly common for related businesses to approach you with special perks, hoping to reach your loyal audience.

Enjoy these benefits aside from your stable source of income from your loyal customers.

Tip 5: This lead magnet type is only a recommendation

The niche tools eReport lead magnet is not a hard requirement. It's only a recommendation. Other lead magnet types also work. Some may even perform better. Webinars and free product trials prove to be more effective at collecting email addresses.

From an efficiency standpoint (i.e., cost to produce vs. impact and effect), the niche tools eReport lead magnet is optimal for beginners with minimal resources who are starting from scratch.

We now have an appreciation for the value of an audience in business. We've also produced a lead magnet that allows us to captivate the niche crowd and build a database of email addresses. It's time to set up the place to facilitate that exchange – a platform that our niche crowd can visit, subscribe to for our lead magnet, and process the delivery of that lead magnet.

Let's get to work on our website.

Chapter 5
The Digital Space between Us

Stage 1 - Audience-Building Machine

*"Domain names and websites are Internet
real estate." – Marc Ostrofsky*

Marking Our Online Territory

"Dun-dun-duuunnn" echoes inside our head as the most dreaded online task, especially for non-techies, looms on the horizon – coding and building our website. It's a terrifying ordeal filled with technical shenanigans and indecipherable language, all of which prevent many entrepreneurs from getting their feet wet online.

Well, not anymore.

Building a website used to be difficult. A technophobe friend of mine even described it as working with an "alien language." Advancements in online technology though, combined with the efforts of the online open source community, have given non-techie entrepreneurs like us the capability to build websites with minimal interaction with computer programming languages.

Securing and building a robust and professional website now involves nothing more than a few clicks, a bit of configuration, and a pinch of imagination. In today's digital world, marking our online territory and having our place on the World Wide Web is both simple and affordable.

We are creating our own website as a venue for our niche crowd to visit – where they can subscribe to download our lead magnet. Our website is the window that facilitates the collection of the subscriber's email address and the delivery of the lead magnet.

Admittedly, we can use ***Facebook Pages*** and other blogging platforms to accomplish the same purpose. However, having our own website gives us the advantage of branding, as well as more control on our website's features. **Kurtroswell.com** inspires more confidence and awe compared to **facebook.com/kurtroswell** or **kurtroswell.typepad.com**, wouldn't you agree?

Now, let's go through the simple process of building our own website, one click at a time.

Our Place on the Web

Having our own website starts with securing our space on the web.

It's easy to think of websites as digital codes that exist in the air, the ether, or Narnia because we don't get to see any physical structures. Websites do live inside specialized computers that are connected to the internet 24/7 – they are called **web servers**.

To carve our own space on a tiny corner of the web, we need to get a **domain name** and a **web hosting service**.

Step 1: Choose an online name

We need to decide on the name we would like to use online. This online name serves as our official name and aims to differentiate us from other experts in the industry.

We can use our real names or create professional pen names. Don't hesitate to use a pen name. Adopting a pen name is a widely-accepted practice in the business and creative fields. This allows us to have a business presence that's independent of our personal lives.

An alternative is to use an avatar. Instead of using your real name, you can use a character or a descriptive title. Think of it as an online persona like *the marketing guru, the love doctor,* or *the fitness mentor*. Just be sure your content lives up to the title you use.

Step 2: Buy the domain name

Once we've chosen an online name, it's time to secure our domain name. A **domain name** is our website's name address – the name (usually starting with www.) that users type in their browsers to reach a website.

Purchasing a domain name is done via **domain registrars**. There are many domain registrars online. I prefer *Namecheap*. They offer a user-friendly interface, affordable prices, and free bundles on domain purchases. *Namecheap* also has great customer service.

1. Visit https://www.namecheap.com/.
2. Search for your chosen online name in the search bar. Remember, spaces are not allowed in domain names.
3. If your chosen online name is available as a domain name, go ahead and purchase it. Domain names vary in price, but a typical domain name costs less than $12 per year. That's a single dollar per month.

Notes for this section

- Don't use hyphens in domain names. Imagine talking to someone and having to say your website address vocally with hyphens. Uttering "kurtroswell dot com, one word" flows smoother than saying "Kurt hyphen Roswell dot com" out loud.
- If your chosen online name is unavailable, you can append your industry. It would look like kurtroswellmarketing.com.
- Stick to **.com** domain name suffixes as much as possible. In the online world, internet users are most comfortable with .com websites, followed by a preference for .net and .org suffixes.

Step 3: Subscribe to a web hosting service

After securing a domain name, we need to subscribe to a web hosting service. **Web hosting** is a utility service that provides online space for storage, processing, and serving our website files to users and visitors. A web hosting service grants your website a room on the web and allows that website to exist online.

For our purpose, which is to set up a website to build an audience, we only need the basic features. I use **Siteground** (https://www.siteground.com/). We can also opt for **Bluehost** (https://www.bluehost.com/).

Both come highly recommended and are trusted by many online entrepreneurs. **Siteground** and **Bluehost** are top of the line when it comes to available features, technology updates, and customer service. Both also come with user-friendly, one-click feature installations.

1. Visit https://www.siteground.com/.
2. Click on the *Wordpress Hosting* selection. We would be talking about **Wordpress** in the future. For now, know that you want a web hosting service that is optimized for Wordpress deployment.
3. Choose the *StartUp package*. The most basic package will suffice. Most starter (i.e., shared web hosting) packages start at $3 to $4 per month with only minor differences.
4. Since you already have a domain name, tick the appropriate button when prompted. Type in the domain name you registered from the previous step.
5. Complete the purchase of your web hosting service.

<u>Notes for this section</u>

- Know the fine print. Web hosting services' monthly prices are <u>discounted for one cycle</u> – usually one year. After that, prices revert to <u>undiscounted</u> normal prices of $8 to $10 per month upon renewal. This is a standard industry practice. Prepare for this added cost when the time comes to renew your subscription.
- As your website grows, you need to move to more powerful and expensive hosting packages. You'll know it's time to migrate to better packages once you notice your website

slowing down significantly. Don't worry about that right now. The basic web hosting packages are sufficient at this point.

Step 4: Link the domain name to the web hosting account

We now have a domain name and a web hosting account. Since we're using separate providers, we need to link them up. This way, when internet users type our domain name on their browsers, the request will find its way to your web hosting account.

Link your domain name and web hosting account by setting up the domain's **nameserver**. Don't worry; it's simpler than it sounds.

1. After registering your web hosting service, you will receive an email confirming your registration. That same email also contains your DNS settings. It's easy to recognize DNS settings. They usually start with NS1 and NS2 or DNS1 and DNS2, followed by some text with your web host company's domain name. DNS settings look like this – **ns1.us44 .siteground.us** and **ns2.us44.siteground.us**.
2. Copy both sets of DNS information.
3. Proceed to your domain registrar and log in to your account. This would be ***Namecheap*** if you followed our example from the previous section.
4. Go to the settings page of the domain name you are trying to configure. In ***Namecheap***, we go to the *domain manager* and click the *manage* button referring to the applicable domain name.
5. Input both DNS information that you copied earlier in their respective DNS text fields, then save your settings. In ***Namecheap***, we can do this in the *nameserver* settings area, selecting *custom DNS* from the drop-down menu, and entering the DNS on their respective text fields.
6. Wait for your updated DNS configuration to propagate throughout the web. This only takes around five to 15 minutes. Nameserver notifications say that it takes 24 hours

because it used to take that long. We have come a long way since then, and things move much faster now.

7. After waiting, open a browser and try to visit your website. That is, type **http://www.yourdomain.com/** in your browser, replace **yourdomain.com** with the domain name you registered. You'll know your configuration worked properly if you see a *spiel page* of your web host company (i.e., ***Siteground*** if you followed this example) instead of a *parked domain page* of your domain registrar (i.e., ***Namecheap***).

8. Congratulations! You now have your own space on the web, even if it is just a bare-bones spiel page. You have secured the foundation on which your website and online business will soon rise.

Notes for this section

- If you didn't receive or can't find a welcome email from your web host company, you could find the DNS information inside your web hosting account. In the worst case, you can contact your web host company's customer support to retrieve the DNS settings information. In ***Siteground***, you can find the DNS settings under your account's *information & settings* tab.

- There's no need to panic if you get confused or stuck at any point. You can always ask your domain registrar's or web hosting company's support team for help. You can also refer to many online resources.

Clicking can Build a Website: Using Wordpress

Now that we have our place in the web, it's time to build our actual website.

There was a time when building your website was hard. I learned HTML and CSS to create my first few websites. I also needed to code a functional website from scratch.

But lo and behold, a gift from the heavens – **Content Management Systems** (or **CMS**) made its way into the online world. With its arrival, creating websites just got a whole lot easier and faster.

CMS is a software tool that allows us to create, manage, design, and publish a blog. Install the CMS software, configure a few settings, and you'll have a fully-functional blog in minutes.

CMS software has since evolved to offer advanced features for creating any type of website imaginable – not just blogs or simple websites. We can now build aesthetically pleasing websites with a full stack of sophisticated functionalities using the latest CMS tools.

Among all CMS brands out there (e.g. ***Drupal***, ***Joomla!***, and ***Magento***), the most popular CMS for online entrepreneurs is ***Wordpress***. We mentioned Wordpress in passing earlier when we were talking about web hosting services. It's time to shed more light on this wonderful software.

Wordpress is the most powerful and versatile, as well as the most-used, CMS for online entrepreneurs. It is open-source – there is an entire collaborative community that supports its development. That's why this CMS software continues to evolve with more powerful capabilities. Open-source also means that the software is free. You have powerful software that can be used for free, what's not to love?

Installing Wordpress on your web hosting account is simple. Getting familiar with it and initializing your website only involves a few configurations here and there, even if you're not a code nerd.

Step 1: Install Wordpress

All web host companies have a *Wordpress easy install* feature with their web hosting packages. Wordpress, as I've said, is the most popular CMS online. Follow any of these installation options.

Option 1: Web hosting account dashboard

If you're using **Siteground**, we can find the *Wordpress installation* shortcut inside your **Siteground** account, under the *installations* tab.

For other web host companies, we can find a similar shortcut on our web hosting account's dashboard.

1. Inside the *WordPress installation* page, indicate the domain name where you want to install Wordpress.
2. Fill in the necessary website information. Don't worry too much, since these settings are all editable – you can still make changes after saving them. Do consider your *Admin Username* and *Password* carefully at this point.
3. For other settings like *Database Name* and *Table Prefix*, you can leave them set to their default values.
4. Hit *install.*

Option 2: cPanel

If we can't find a *Wordpress installation* shortcut on the web hosting account dashboard, we can access the **cPanel** to find the Wordpress installer button there.

Don't panic. **cPanel** is simply software for managing web hosting accounts and websites. It provides an appealing graphical user interface (GUI). All website operators are familiar with this web hosting management software, so the chances are great that your web host company adopts cPanel as well.

We can access cPanel by logging into our web hosting account dashboard and clicking on the *cPanel* shortcut. Alternatively, we can visit cPanel by going to **http://www.yourdomain.com/cpanel** – change **yourdomain.com** to the domain we registered. Our web hosting account and its respective cPanel share the same username and password by default.

We'll then go through the same *Wordpress installation* process as above.

Option 3: Seek help from the web host company's customer support

If we want to skip all the particulars of a Wordpress installation altogether, we can go straight to the web host company's customer support. They'll ask us for some information about the installation, and we'll have Wordpress installed on our domain name in three minutes or less.

Step 2: Understand the Wordpress dashboard

After installing Wordpress, it's time to access the *Wordpress dashboard*.

By default, we can access the WordPress dashboard by visiting **http://www.yourdomain.com/wp-login.php**, do change **your domain.com** to your domain name. We then log in using the *admin username* and *password* we chose during the Wordpress installation.

The WordPress dashboard is our main control center for running our entire website – from changing the website design to writing and publishing a blog post.

The interface is intuitive. The major functionalities we will use regularly are located on the left panel. Feel free to familiarize yourself with the interface and tinker with the configurations.

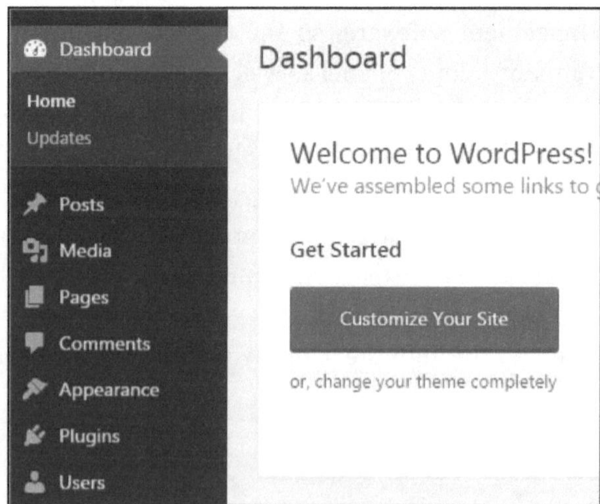

Several key functionalities are worth discussing. These functionalities can confuse most people, especially first-timers. We need to be clear about the difference between *Themes* (located in the *Appearance* tab) vs. *Plugins,* as well as the difference between *Posts* vs. *Pages.*

Key functionality 1: Themes vs. Plugins

Both *themes* and *plugins* are downloadable packages or files that we can install on our Wordpress website. We install them via their respective *Add New* buttons.

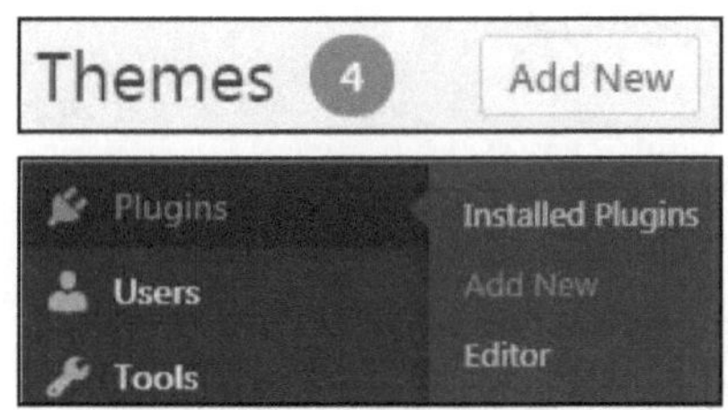

Themes control the overall appearance of your website – the layout, design, colors, font designs, font sizes, bullet points, and the available widget slots.

Plugins, on the other hand, extend added functionalities to our website – functionalities that don't come by default with Wordpress. These functionalities can include additional security, e-commerce capabilities, backup mechanisms, website analytics, and a host of other powerful functions.

There are boatloads of free *themes* and *plugins* available inside the Wordpress directory. There are also premium *themes* and *plugins* that you can buy from independent developers.

Key functionality 2: Posts vs. Pages

Both *posts* and *pages* represent content on our website. On the surface, *posts* and *pages* appear the same. However, knowing the subtle differences between the two enables you to use the correct type depending on your needs.

Posts are made of timely content – they have listed *dates* by default. We can also add descriptive *tags* and *categories* to *posts*. They are also listed in reverse chronological order (the newest *posts* go at the top) in our *posts page*, as illustrated below. We use *posts* to publish blog entries like news and updates on our website.

Pages are timeless, one-off, and static content on our website. Static content common to most websites includes the *Privacy Policy page*, *Terms and Conditions page*, and the *Contact Us page*, as well as the *About Us page*. Website owners also use *pages* to create product pages, media kit pages, and in most cases, the home page – the front page of the website.

Notes for this section

- When selecting a *theme*, choose one that is <u>responsive</u>. Responsive themes mean that the design adapts well to any size of the screen. The website elements and sections rearrange and stack up to look pleasant. Images also automatically resize to fit and look beautiful when viewed from any device.

- The **posts page**, otherwise known as the **blog index page**, lists our website's blog post summaries in reverse chronological order. The most recent blog post will appear at the top. Users can click on the post title to go to the post itself.
- The front page, more commonly known as the home page, is the page that shows up when users go to http://www.YOUR DOMAIN.com/.

Step 3: Set up the front page

A website's **front page** is that website's most valuable real estate. Most visitors arrive at the front page first, and they navigate through the rest of the website from there. It's the first page (and may be the only page) that most visitors will see and interact with.

Most websites have their *posts page* as their front page. This is especially true with blogs. Being a CMS originally designed for blogging, Wordpress is configured to set the *posts page* as the front page by default.

We are following a specific business model here – with the primary purpose of building an audience. To achieve that, we want to use the highly-valuable front page as a powerful email-capturing device, so we capture more of our visitors' emails, serve our lead magnet, and build our audience faster.

We need to set up our website to display a *static page* (i.e., a typical WordPress page) on our front page, instead of the default *posts page*.

Sub-step 1: Create a page

Since our website doesn't have any real content – neither *posts* nor *pages* – yet, the first thing we need to do is create a *page*. Once we have a *page*, we can configure it to serve as our *front page*.

1. On the WordPress dashboard, find the *Pages* tab on the left panel.
2. Under the *Pages* tab, click *Add New*.

3. You'll find yourself in the **WordPress content editor**.
    Add a descriptive title to the top text field where it says *Enter
    title here*.
4. Click the *Publish* button on the right.
5. Congratulations, you have just created your very first *page*.

Sub-step 2: Set new page as front page

Once we have a *page*, we can now configure it to become our
front page.

1. On the WordPress dashboard, find the *Settings* tab on the
    left panel.
2. Under the *Settings* tab, click on *Reading*.
3. Focus on the *Front page displays* settings. By default, the
    radio button is indicated as *Your latest posts*. This means
    your *posts page* is currently the *front page*. Select the *A
    static page (select below)* radio button instead.
4. Two drop-down fields will appear – *Front page* and *Posts
    page*. On the *Front page* settings, click the drop-down menu,
    and select the *page* you created earlier. This is now the front
    page of your website.
5. Well done. You now have a static front page. It's still blank
    right now, but it's ripe for building and customization.

<u>Notes for this section</u>

•   There is a sample *post*, a sample *page*, and a sample
    comment that come with each fresh Wordpress installation.
    We can delete those since they are just sample placeholders
    to show the appearance of each type of content when
    published.
•   For the title of the *page* we created in this section, it's
    advisable to use the title of our lead magnet. We are using
    this specific page as an email-capturing device for our lead
    magnet after all.
•   We can manage all the *pages* we have created by going to
    Pages ➜ *All Pages* in the left panel.

- Each time we create a *page* or a *post*, Wordpress assigns a **URL (Uniform Resource Locator)** for that particular content. A **URL**, otherwise known as the **page address**, **permalink**, or **slug**, is that content's exact location on the web. Users can type or copy this URL text string into any browser and go straight to this content, even without clicking through links or going through redirects. The URL appears below the *title* text field after we've entered a title for this content. We can click on *edit* to make any necessary changes.

- We can configure the new location of our posts page in the *Posts page* field under *Settings* ➔ *Reading* ➔ *Front page displays* ➔ *Posts page*. This is useful if we decide to start a blog on our website.

Powerful Squeeze Pages: Using Wordpress Content Editor

Wordpress has a default theme set up with each fresh installation. Right now, if we install a different theme package, our entire website would adopt that theme's settings. That's okay. It is how themes are supposed to work.

To build our audience, we are going to use the WordPress content editor to create a powerful email-capturing device – a **squeeze page**.

The WordPress content editor is a built-in editor used to input and edit the main content of every post or page. Every new post or page we create opens up the WordPress content editor – where we write, format, add images, code, schedule, and publish what goes in a particular post or page.

A **squeeze page** is any page designed to funnel and squeeze visitors into doing only a single action – one of our choosing – on that page.

One prominent characteristic of a good squeeze page is the lack of distracting elements – links to other pages, advertisements, and even, navigation menus.

The idea is to leave as little option as possible for the visitor to take any action other than the one we want them to take. For our audience-building machine, the action we want our visitors to take is to subscribe to our lead magnet, submit their email addresses, and become part of our audience.

A squeeze page contains only content – text, images, audios, or videos – designed to entice, influence, and persuade the visitors into the intended action. It is capped off with a button or form so that users can take the intended action. This can be a *buy now* button that leads to a check-out process or, for our email-capturing purposes, an email opt-in form to collect contact information from the visitor.

Building pages for impact

What we put on our squeeze page is dependent on our niche, our lead magnet, and the value we are trying to offer our visitors. Each situation is different, so I can't show you exactly what page design to create, what compelling statements to write, or what attention-grabbing images to include. That is entirely up to you.

What I can do is equip you with the right tools, resources, and tips to create the common elements of the squeeze page easily.

Element 1: Page sections

Page section refers to our page's overall layout and different components. We use the WordPress content editor to build our page section by section.

A word of caution, the built-in editor that comes with Wordpress is intuitive, but it is weak. Although it's described as a WYSIWYG (i.e., What You See Is What You Get) editor, it behaves more like a "What You See Is What You <u>Might</u> Get" disaster. The

WordPress content editor is also not robust enough to create advanced elements like icon boxes, sophisticated buttons, or designed sections without using code.

Lucky for us, there are downloadable plugins that enhance the WordPress content editor to give it powerful features. Some editor plugins even overwrite the native Wordpress content editor entirely.

I use the **Thrive Themes** suite of tools (https://www.thrive themes.com/). This toolbox contains an editor called **Thrive Architect**. This editor enables robust page-building via a drag-and-drop interface. Without touching code, we can insert call to action buttons, opt-in forms, testimonial boxes, social share buttons, and animated countdown timers on the page simply by dragging and dropping.

Thrive Themes is a paid product. While it is affordable for the number of tools and continuous upgrades it provides, you may be working with minimal resources. Keep Thrive Themes in mind for future consideration for now. It can level up your page creation ability significantly.

A free alternative to Thrive Themes is the **Elementor Page Builder** plugin (https://wordpress.org/plugins/elementor/). It's the closest to Thrive Themes in terms of ease of use and capabilities – it only differs on a few non-critical features.

1. We can install this plugin, or any plugin for that matter, by going to the *Plugins* tab located on WordPress dashboard's left panel then clicking *Add New*.
2. Search for *Elementary Page Builder* and look for it in the search results.
3. Click *Install Now*.
4. Once installed, *activate* the Elementor Page Builder plugin.

Element 2: Text

Text content is every word, phrase, sentence, and statement that makes up your website. For the squeeze page, keep in mind that we are trying to entice the reader to download our lead magnet. Every statement we write should work toward that goal.

Text content that aims to persuade the reader to take a specific action is known as a **sales copy**, or simply **copy**.

Lead magnet copy is a great place to begin learning the skill of copywriting. It's more sophisticated than ad copy, yet less intimidating than full-blown product sales copy. To write an effective lead magnet copy, we need to emphasize two things – articulating **pain points** and painting **pleasure points**.

Pain points refer to our niche crowd's problems, issues, and concerns. These pain points are the source of our niche crowd's suffering. We refer to our niche crowd research to give us insights into our niche crowd's psyche. We then verbalize those pain points to go into our lead magnet copy.

As for **pleasure points**, we will use them to paint a vivid picture of what life would be like – more specifically, how pleasant it would be – once the pain point is gone.

It's advisable to use **features** (i.e., a five-page eBook, learn five secrets, downloadable, readable via mobile, etc.) and **benefits** (i.e., more monthly income, more free time for yourself, better health, etc.) in tandem when writing lead magnet copy. Mention benefits before mentioning any features and use more benefits than features.

Element 3: Images

Images bring focus to specific sections of our page. Your reader's attention naturally gravitates to interesting images rather than blocks of text. You need to break the gray wall of text to keep your readers engaged.

Images also serve as visual breaks for the reader's eyes, giving them relief from reading too much text at once.

A great source for free and high-quality images is *Pixabay* (https://www.pixabay.com/). It features a search engine that helps us find images relevant to our lead magnet's message.

We might also want to use desktop screenshots for our squeeze page. The best tool for generating and editing screenshot images is *LightShot* (https://app.prntscr.com/en/index.html). LightShot is a lightweight download that is installed on your desktop computer.

Once installed, we can click on the *Print Screen* key on our keyboard to take and edit screenshots. It's that easy and user-friendly.

<u>Notes for this section</u>

- Keep this mindset while building squeeze pages – entice, convince, and persuade visitors into the action we want them to take. Every element should build toward that goal. Unnecessary elements should be removed.

- Plugins and themes need to be activated before they become fully-functional on your website. Find the plugins list (*Plugins* → *Installed Plugins*) or themes list (*Appearance* → *Themes*) on the left panel of the Wordpress dashboard. You can then *activate* your plugins and themes from there.

- Relevance is worth emphasizing here. The lead magnet copy and the images you use are meant to "sell" your specific lead magnet. Make sure only to include text and image elements that align with your specific lead magnet.

- Benchmark. Look at what's already working in your niche. Use that as a starting point. When writing lead magnet copy, refer to the websites of other influencers. Examine how they articulate the **pain** and **pleasure points** for their niche crowds. Benchmarking <u>does not</u> mean copying or plagiarizing! Use benchmarks as a basis to know what's working as well as a starting point for your writing, but write your own copy.

Components of an effective squeeze page

Squeeze pages can come in all shapes and sizes. For a while, "above the fold" squeeze pages – pages wherein all content is viewable without the need to scroll down – dominated the web.

Now, we get to see more and more squeeze pages adopting the design aesthetics of modern business websites and blogs – a big image with one main benefit statement covers most of the above the fold section, followed below by the other components of the squeeze page when the visitor scrolls down. Brian Harris's ***VideoFruit*** (https://www.videofruit.com/) is a great example.

Both design principles are effective ways to entice our visitors to download our lead magnet and capture their email addresses. Regardless of what squeeze page design you choose to follow, every effective squeeze page contains several key components.

Component 1: Story

Stories are powerful ways to connect with visitors – sharing an emotional or a success story related to the lead magnet or niche topic is very powerful. We can share a short story about our struggles. We can also state how we used the tips and tools inside the lead magnet to overcome those challenges. A more relatable story increases the chance that our visitors will download our lead magnet.

Component 2: Benefit boxes or bullets

An organized, bite-sized list of benefits can help a visitor determine the value of your lead magnet easily. Reading through the powerful benefits of our lead magnet helps our visitors decide if downloading it is worth their time.

Component 3: Social proof

Social proof includes the logos of big brands, famous organizations, or media appearances we have worked with. If recognized institutions have featured our work, we include those as well. Endorsements from influential people are also useful here. The idea is to project credibility by association.

Since we are starting from scratch, we can use testimonials from colleagues. We just need to make sure that their testimonials are relevant to our niche. We also need to remember the need to build up our social proof credentials as we gain a better foothold in our niche.

Component 4: Call to action buttons or opt-in forms

Call to action buttons, and **opt-in forms** represent the interactive elements of our squeeze page. This is where the visitors enter their email addresses, press the *submit* button, and receive our lead magnet.

Generating buttons and opt-in forms are easy, despite the many processes happening behind the scenes. Ever wondered where the email address goes or how the lead magnet gets delivered? It's a series of coordinated processes made automatic by wonderful software – the **email marketing app**.

Notes for this section

- If you choose to put a navigation menu in your squeeze page, place it near the bottom of the page. Doing so increases the focus on your lead magnet instead of getting tempted to visit other pages.

- Remember that if you don't ask, your visitors will never do it. So include some copy around the call to action button or the opt-in form. You can't expect the visitors to intuitively know what you want them to do. A simple "enter your best email address below and click submit to gain access," followed by the opt-in form, can go a long way. You need to keep it simple – suggest the action you want them to take.

- Consider putting multiple call to action buttons or opt-in forms throughout the squeeze page. Of course, don't overdo it.

- Every output or asset you release (from a web page, a blog post, an email, a social media post, a book, a workshop, a product, etc.) into the world should have some sort of call to action for the readers or viewers to take. The call to action should build your business, whether it is a simple invitation for your readers to follow you on social media or a complex action like asking for a sale. Output with no call to action is a wasted opportunity.

Assemble Our Audience: Using an Email Marketing App

An **email marketing app** is a program that allows us to collect visitors' email addresses, organize our contacts, send out customized email blasts, and automate the entire process. This is also known as an **email marketing software** or **autoresponder**.

This software facilitates the email marketing tasks that allow us to build an audience and engage them in continuous discussion beyond our website. On our website, the manifestation of the email marketing app is the call to action button or opt-in form.

The email marketing app is different from our personal email service provider like *Gmail*, *Yahoo! Mail*, or *Hotmail*. Email marketing apps contain features that are suitable for business purposes. Imagine using a *Gmail* account to send an email to our audience of five to 20 people. It's easy, right?

It is more difficult to do the same thing for an audience of 500, 5,000, 10,000, and beyond. This is where we need the automation offered by an email marketing app.

This software allows us to send bulk emails to our sizable audience as if we were emailing each one of them personally. The email marketing app also allows us to collect the email addresses of our visitors and manage the subscribers easily.

Other features include sending out pre-scheduled emails in a series (i.e., an email series), sending out emails to a sub-segment of our audience based on set criteria, and tracking user behaviors – like email opens and clicks.

Step 1: Subscribe to an email marketing app

The email marketing app is the most vital cog in our entire make-money-online machine – since it holds our list of email addresses and facilitates audience building. There are many email marketing providers out there to give us robust email marketing capabilities at affordable prices. Among email marketing providers, I recommend these services.

Recommendation 1: Mailchimp (<ins>https://www.mailchimp.com/</ins>)

Mailchimp is the best email marketing app provider <ins>for beginners</ins>. It offers a free plan for up to 2,000 subscribers. While there are feature limitations to the free plan, *Mailchimp* allows us to test the waters and familiarize ourselves with email marketing without spending.

Recommendation 2: AWeber (<ins>https://www.aweber.com/</ins>)

AWeber is one of the most popular email marketing app providers for Online Marketers. They offer a user-friendly interface and boast one of the highest email deliverability rates in the industry. *AWeber* has long been the industry standard for email marketing apps.

Recommendation 3: ActiveCampaign (<ins>https://www.active campaign.com/</ins>), ConvertKit (<ins>https://wwws.convertkit.com/</ins>), and Drip (<ins>https://www.drip.co/</ins>)

These three are emerging email marketing apps. They are a bit more expensive, but they contain advanced features that can level up any email marketing campaign.

ActiveCampaign gives us the power to execute email marketing automation magic like a pro with ease, using a visual drag-and-drop flow diagram.

ConvertKit packs features that used to be available only to enterprise-level providers.

Drip is a platform that is exploring new horizons by providing features beyond email like *Facebook Lead Ads* integration and user web activity tracking.

Any of these email marketing apps can help us create sophisticated online campaigns.

I use *Drip* as my email marketing app. It's the perfect blend of simplicity, cost, and advanced features. It's also great for getting familiar with email marketing apps since it offers a free plan (like Mailchimp) for up to 100 subscribers.

Once you've decided on an email marketing app to use, we can proceed to create and configure the call to action buttons or email opt-in forms for our lead magnet squeeze page. We'll be using Mailchimp to illustrate this process since it's the most accessible to beginners.

The underlying principles and processes, though, are similar across all email marketing apps.

Step 2: Make our lead magnet downloadable

Before we go setting up necessary buttons or opt-in forms on our lead magnet squeeze page, we need to host our lead magnet online. That way, our lead magnet can be downloaded via a link, so we don't have to email the lead magnet to the subscriber manually.

We can host our lead magnet on our website or use a free online file hosting service like **Google Drive** or **Dropbox**.

Option 1: Self-host on website

Hosting your lead magnet on your website gives you control and ambient branding, but self-hosting consumes your web hosting resources whenever a user downloads the lead magnet.

1. Log in to your website's Wordpress dashboard.
2. Go to the *Media* tab on the left control panel, click *Add New*.
3. Drag your lead magnet file to the *Drop files here* box.
4. Once uploaded, select the lead magnet from the list, copy the location of the lead magnet file as indicated on the *URL* field on the right side. This is your lead magnet's download link.

Option 2: File hosting service

Using a file hosting service like **Google Drive** or **Dropbox** offers security and spares your website's resources. Doing this, though, is more tedious to set up and relinquishes some of your control. The process below is for **Google Drive**.

1. Log in to your Google Drive account.
2. Upload your lead magnet file.

3. Once uploaded, *Right Click* on the lead magnet icon and click the *Share…* button.
4. Copy the URL location of the lead magnet file. This is your lead magnet's download link.

<u>Notes for this section</u>

- Whenever you publish your lead magnet download link, you need to instruct the users to *Right Click + Save As* to download it. Most web browsers now open the lead magnet in a new browser window by default. There's nothing wrong with this, but we prefer to have our visitors download the lead magnet to their computers or devices rather than read it online. This way, our subscribers get to keep a copy of it in case they lose the lead magnet's download link.

Step 3: Automate collection and delivery

Now that we have our lead magnet download link, it's time to configure our email marketing app for automation. We automate the collection of email addresses from subscribers and the immediate delivery of the lead magnet to those subscribers. The process involves **creating a list** then configuring the **welcome email**.

Sub-step 1: Create the list

In email marketing apps, **lists** represent the repository for subscribers' collected contact information, as well as the tools enabling us to collect and manage those email addresses. These tools within **lists** include **contact managers** and **signup form builders**.

The instructions below use MailChimp, though the principles apply to other email marketing apps as well.

1. Log in to your email marketing app account.
2. Go to the *Create List* function.

3. Fill up the necessary list details. These are the fields available for MailChimp lists.

- o **List name**. This is the title of your list. Make this descriptive, since your subscribers would be able to see this.
- o **From email address**. This is the email address from which your emails are sent. This should be a real email address since MailChimp sends a verification email to this address. Your subscriber also replies to this email address.
- o **From Name**. This is the name that will appear on your subscriber's inbox when they receive your emails. Just enter the pen name you chose so that subscribers can recognize you instantly.
- o **Remind people how they signed up to your list**. This is a short description for this list. It's also good to add the benefit statement to this description, to remind the subscriber why they are on your list in the first place. This field is also known as **List Description** in other email marketing apps.

Sub-step 2: Configure the welcome email

Once we've created our **list**, it's time to configure a **welcome email** to greet the new subscribers. The **welcome email** is the automated email sent immediately after a user subscribes to this particular list.

For our audience-building purposes, we will also use the **welcome email** to deliver our lead magnet automatically to our subscribers. We are going to insert the lead magnet download link that we created earlier into the welcome email. This process is specific to MailChimp, but the principle extends to other email marketing apps.

1. Go to *Campaigns* on the main tabs at the top. Mailchimp uses the term **campaigns** to refer to sending email functionalities, among other things.

2. Click on the *Create Campaign* button on the middle right.

3. Select *Create an Email* at the bottom of the pop up.

4. Choose *Automated* from the top tabs. Select *Welcome new subscribers* on the bottom.

5. Type a *campaign name*. The title of your lead magnet is a good descriptive campaign name.

6. Select the list you created earlier from the *Select a list* dropdown. Click *Begin*.

7. You are taken to Mailchimp's **automation builder** screen. This is where you can create emails that are sent automatically to subscribers. For now, there is only one email in this workflow. You can click on the *Add Email* button to add more emails to this workflow to create an email series.

8. For now, we are only concerned about the first email. We want this email to get triggered and sent *immediately* after the visitor subscribes. Do this by clicking *Edit trigger* on that first email and from the *day(s)* dropdown, select *immediately*. Click on *Update Trigger* on the top right to save. This will become the welcome email sent immediately after subscription.

9. We now need to edit the content of this email. Click on *Design Email*.

10. Input the necessary details as you like. For the *Email subject*, I suggest using *Here you go, <Title of Your Lead Magnet>*.

11. Select a template for your welcome email as you like. *Simple Text* is usually enough, especially for beginners.

12. You can write your welcome email as you wish. Just make sure to include your lead magnet download link in the email. Here's a sample welcome email with lead magnet download link you can follow. You can click on *Merge Tags* in the email editor to fill dynamic fields like *subscriber's first name*.

****

SUBJECT LINE:
Here you go, *<Title of Your Lead Magnet>*

BODY:
Hey *<Subscriber's First Name>*,

Thank you so much for your interest in my eReport "*<Title of You Lead Magnet>*."

<u>Click here to download the eReport</u> ← *<insert lead magnet download link here>*

The eReport is a short read but if you have been struggling to *<insert problems, issues, and concerns that your lead magnet can solve>*, "*<Title of Your Lead Magnet>*" can change your paradigm and results.

I hope you enjoy it – let me know what you think!

Cheers

<Your Pen Name> – Author of "*<Title of Your Lead Magnet>*"

P.S. I love hearing about success stories, so do email me and share the insights you got from the eReport.
****

13. Click on *Save and Continue* at the bottom right to save this email.
14. Going back to Mailchimp's automation builder screen, click on *Next* at the bottom right to review your newly-created campaign. Resolve any issue that may come up. Click on *Email details* to see the issues within the email.

15. Once all issues are resolved, click the *Start Workflow* button at the bottom right. This saves and runs this workflow.

What we just did was automate the process of email address collection and lead magnet delivery. Now, every time a visitor subscribes on our squeeze page, their contact information goes to our list. The subscriber automatically receives this welcome email, with the lead magnet download link inside, and they can now download the lead magnet without our intervention.

<u>Notes for this section</u>

- Email marketing apps may use different terminologies for their functionalities. The core principles for these functionalities, though, are the same for all of them.
- While MailChimp offers generous features with their free account, their interface is a bit unintuitive. Other email marketing apps offer a simpler interface and workflow.
- If any part of the process is unclear, you can rely on your email marketing app's customer support or video demos to guide you further.

Step 4: Integrate an opt-in form into the squeeze page

We have properly set up our email marketing app to collect subscriber email addresses and deliver our lead magnet on autopilot.

It is now time to integrate a call to action button or email opt-in form on our squeeze page. The opt-in form is where visitors to our squeeze page enter their email address, press the submit button, subscribe to our lead magnet, and become part of our audience.

The implementation of the call to action button or email opt-in form is dependent on what platform you use to create that opt-in form. In most cases, it's possible for either the theme/plugin or the email marketing app to create the opt-in form.

Scenario 1: Theme or plugin API connection

Some Wordpress themes and plugins have buttons and forms with built-in integrations for popular email marketing apps. ***Thrive***

Themes is one suite of tools that has this kind of strong integration. We simply connect the tool's settings to our email marketing app.

This is done using an *API connection* (Application Programming Interface connection) – the technical term for the way software and apps talk to each other. Refer to your tool's (whether it's a theme or a plugin) documentations and settings to configure yours correctly.

Scenario 2: Email marketing app embedded forms

In the worst case, our Wordpress theme or content editor plugin doesn't have any opt-in form integrations.

If this is so, we must create the call to action button or email opt-in form from the email marketing app side. Within each list inside our email marketing app lies the ability to create forms for that list.

1. For MailChimp, go to *Lists* on the main tabs at the top.
2. Choose the list you want to create an opt-in form for from the lineup.
3. In the tabs along the middle section, choose *Signup forms* ➜ *Embedded forms*. **Embedded forms** are forms that can be inserted on different parts of your website. Creating embedded forms generates a code that can be copied and pasted to sections of our squeeze page where we want the forms to appear.
4. Configure the form and copy the embed code.
5. Paste this embed code on sections of your squeeze page where you want the form to appear.

Notes for this section

- The embedded form's embed code is in HTML (Hypertext Markup Language) format – the display language of the web. Inserting HTML code on a web page is dependent on the theme or plugin we choose to use. Refer to your theme or plugin's documentation to see how it handles HTML. In most cases, we can see the HTML code of a WordPress page or post from the content editor. While editing that post or page using the content editor, switch to *Code Editor* instead of the *Visual Editor* via the settings (button with three vertical dots) located on the top right section. You are now looking at this page's HTML code.

Stage 1 - Audience-Building Machine: Wrap-Up and Pro Tips

Following the instructions laid out in this chapter, we will build a squeeze page with its own domain name and web hosting service. This squeeze page is designed to entice visitors to subscribe and download our lead magnet – a process facilitated by our chosen email marketing app.

Once set up, the machine automates the audience-building process – edifying the lead magnet, collecting the email address, delivering the lead magnet, and managing our email list (i.e., your audience).

Before proceeding further, here are audience-building best practices to consider.

Tip 1: Test before launching

Before launching (i.e., going live and getting visitors to our website), we need to make sure that our audience-building machine runs smoothly. It's a good idea to sign up on our opt-in form and go through the same process our visitors are expected to go through.

After subscribing, check that the welcome email arrives in our inbox immediately. Test the link inside the welcome email and download the lead magnet. Making sure that the process works properly is the best way to avoid missed opportunities and wasted potential subscribers.

Tip 2: Purchase the email marketing app last

At the start, the email marketing app is the most expensive component of our Agile Online Income Machine – it costs about $20 per month.

We work on our lead magnet and website first. Once we are ready to integrate the opt-in form into our website, we can purchase the email marketing app then proceed to launch our website.

Tip 3: Name and email address are enough

Asking for our visitors' first names and email addresses is enough. Requiring more information from our visitors may lead to a significant drop in sign-ups. In some cases, Online Marketers go as far as only asking for email addresses. I leave this to your discretion. Keep in mind that the more information we ask for, the more burden we put on the visitor, and the likelihood of that visitor signing up with us drop accordingly.

Tip 4: Follow double opt-in laws

Double opt-in means that when visitors subscribe, they need to confirm that subscription before becoming active subscribers. This is instituted to prevent SPAM (i.e., marketers getting hold of an email address and emailing the owner without permission) and to verify that the visitor indeed chose to subscribe willingly.

This works by sending a **confirmation email** that a subscriber needs to verify before activating the ability to receive further emails (i.e., before the subscriber gets our welcome email and other succeeding emails). The subscriber can verify their intent to join our email list by clicking on a link inside that confirmation email.

An important thing to understand is that a double opt-in setup is required in some countries. This requirement is stricter now that the EU implemented their GDPR (General Data Protection Regulation) rules a while back. If you aren't sure about going for a double opt-in setup or not, lean on the safe side and implement it.

Setting up a double opt-in is a feature carried by all email marketing apps. Keep in mind that confirmation emails for double opt-in will add another hoop for our visitors to jump through, and that can lower the rate of subscription.

Tip 5: Don't wait for perfect

Reid Hoffman said, "if you're not mortally embarrassed by the quality of your initial release, you released too late."

For us, it means that we mustn't wait for perfection before launching. As long as our machine has complete components that work properly, we should launch. We can make adjustments to improve the system along the way.

The web hosting service and email marketing app stay usable, even if we choose to change niches or start over. The domain name is the only real loss with each pivot to a different niche. If we choose to use the same domain name, then we can pivot without any additional cost.

Tip 6: LeadPages as a shortcut

If we so choose, we can skip the technicalities of building our own squeeze page by using **Leadpages** (https://www.leadpages .net/).

LeadPages, in essence, creates our squeeze page for us without needing to deal with web hosting services, Wordpress configurations, or web page design. All we need to do is integrate our email marketing app (i.e., the email marketing app is <u>not</u> included in **LeadPages**), and we're set to build our audience.

The trade-off for this speed and convenience is cost. LeadPages will consume a big chunk of our monthly budget. Still, it's one of the best options if we don't want to deal with the technical side of building a website.

Once we have our audience-building machine up and running smoothly, it's time to release it into the world. The adage "build it and they will come" doesn't apply here, though – we will need to work to get subscribers to come to us. We need to attract visitors to our website. This is a practice known as traffic generation, which we will work on next.

Chapter 6
Start the Engines

Traffic Generation

"Don't forget: when you start a website, it's not yet a trusted site. So you have to bring people from a trusted site to your site to build up the trust in your site." – James Altucher

The Lifeblood of Our Online Business

"If a tree falls in a forest and no one is around to hear it, does it make a sound?" An interviewer asked me this question back in college when I was applying for an executive position in a school organization. It was a weird question for an interview but it does merit some deep thought.

We can think along the same line with websites and our online business. A website with no visitors does not "make a sound" and might as well not exist at all. With no visitors, there's no way our Agile Online Income Machine can generate income and grant us financial freedom. The solution, then, is to learn how to attract visitors by generating traffic.

Traffic is the lifeblood of any business. It is the component that makes our money-making machine run. Traffic is akin to the blood running through our veins or the fuel that enables an engine to function. Without these, there is nothing but an empty shell that remains lifeless – a shiny, powerful engine that does not move. The absence of traffic to a website means that all we have is a fully functional but invisible web presence.

You'll hear the statement "content is king" sooner or later. I'll contest this and say <u>traffic</u> is the real king.

We can have an ugly, messy website muddled with crappy content, but, with enough traffic, it is possible to make a sale and produce income. Even if it has a minuscule chance of 1 in 10,000, enough traffic can make at least one sale possible.

On the flip side, a perfect website with perfect content but zero visitors will never make a sale. Perfection multiplied by zero is still zero.

When it comes to generating traffic, there are many methods available out there. From free to paid, cold to warm, disinterested to qualified, it's a veritable smorgasbord of techniques to catch an online user's attention and lure them into our website.

We are operating from a unique position – we are starting from absolute scratch with zero influence, authority, and offline presence. Add the fact that we are working on scarce money and time resources.

Let's consider these as I share the most effective traffic generation methods that best fit our unique starting point, one that is also aligned to achieving our specific goal.

Attracting an Audience from Nothing

A floppity-jillion traffic generation methods and platforms from a gazillion sources – this is what we're facing in the Online Marketing space. From the articles of our favorite blogs, to serendipitous shares that pop up on our timelines, all the way to those unsolicited promotional emails – we will always come across material that attempts to hook us on the next groundbreaking traffic generation method.

Some of those methods work for businesses with big audiences. Others work only with big budgets. A whole lot more are outright bogus. This avalanche of traffic strategies and tactics means we need to sift through the many traffic generation methods to find those that work for a business that is starting from scratch.

We need to focus on **seed traffic**, which consists of promotional methods that we can depend on every time we need to attract an audience. This type of traffic does not need special conditions. It also requires minimal resources. We don't need to have an advertising budget, proprietary tools, or an existing audience to execute any given seed traffic technique.

In that sense, seed traffic methods are ideal for businesses that are starting out. These methods may feel like a grind. They feel like we are building our audience person by person. Yet, even in the worst of situations, we can always rely on seed traffic methods to move our online business forward.

Seed traffic method 1: Inner circle

When any entrepreneur starts a venture, the first promotional move out of the gate is to tell family and friends about it.

Essentially, the entrepreneur is banking on the love and respect of family and friends to jumpstart the business. If one is fortunate, that initial love and respect can be enough to trigger a word-of-mouth miracle that will give traction to said business.

In our case, it's also a good idea to start with our immediate circle of family, friends, and acquaintances as we build the foundation for our business. However, while most entrepreneurs begin and end with begging for *likes* to their Facebook business pages, we are building a more qualified audience.

Ask our inner circle to *like* our business page, and we'll receive pity *likes* and token responses. What we want is an audience that is genuinely interested in the asset we are building and the value we are offering. We have to qualify our inner circle very meticulously.

Step 1: Consolidate the inner circle

Our inner circle refers to people who know and interact with us. We can include acquaintances if they fit the description. This means no picking up a cold contact from a business card dropped in a fishbowl with no prior interaction with the person.

1. Go through your mobile phone contacts and list down **100 friends** you've communicated with.
2. Check your emails and take note of **100 people** from your most recent email conversations.
3. Sift through all your social media accounts and tally your **closest 100 friends** for each account.

Step 2: Catch up and confirm interest

After compiling a list of people for our inner circle, we can contact each person to gauge their interest on our niche topic. The idea is to qualify and seek their permission to include them in our audience.

1. Reach out to your contact and do a little catch-up.
2. Once all caught up, send this message – *"I'm working on a new project about <niche topic>. I just thought it might be something you would like. Want in?"* You can personalize this message as you see fit.
3. For those who responded **yes**, ask for their best email address.
4. Inform them that you'll keep in touch with updates.

Step 3: Load the qualified email addresses

Once we've filtered the family, friends, and acquaintances who are interested in our project, we can load their email addresses into our email marketing app.

1. Log in to your email marketing app.
2. Import the email addresses to your campaign.
3. Send a thank you email with your lead magnet attached.
4. Wait for three days. Then send an email asking for feedback about the lead magnet. You should also subtly ask for referrals to people who might also benefit from the lead magnet.

Congratulations, a qualified list of your inner circle is now part of your audience eagerly waiting for what you have to offer.

Notes for this section

- Don't ask your inner circle to share your lead magnet. Instead, ask their referrals to visit your lead magnet squeeze page instead. This is how you will be able to collect their email addresses by signing-up.

Seed traffic method 2: Niche forum engagement

Forums are valuable resources in the online world. These websites specialize in facilitating discussions among the members of its community. Typically, a forum revolves around a specific niche topic. The niche forum then divides into the several subtopic pages, called **threads**, of that niche. This structure allows in-depth discussions across a wide range of niche subtopics.

We can join forums related to our niche and engage with the community, participate in discussions, and help with other members' issues and concerns. In the process, we are letting a qualified crowd of people to get to know us. Eventually, the value we provide to our community gets the members interested in joining our audience base.

Step 1: Search for quality niche forums

Not all forums are created equal. To maximize productivity, it's best to get involved with a few quality forums instead of spending time on a lot of inferior ones.

1. Visit https://www.google.com/.
2. Perform a search using your niche keywords while appending **+forum** at the end of the search phrase. It is also advisable to enclose your niche keywords with quotation marks to perform an exact phrase search. Your searches should appear this way – *"your niche keyword"+forum.*
3. Examine the results and visit the relevant forums. Forums have a distinct appearance – they look like message boards organized into many subtopics.

4. Take note of quality niche forums. We are looking for a substantial number of fresh posts made <u>today</u> or <u>yesterday</u>. The more recent posts that the forum has, the more active the members are. Aside from relevance, active members indicate a quality forum. The number of members is not as important as how active they are. Some niches have small audience populations, and we can expect the forums on that niche to reflect this same member sizes.

Step 2: Join qualified forums and edit your signature settings

Once we've compiled a list of quality niche forums, it's time to filter the ones that are qualified for our traffic generation purposes. We are looking for forums that allow **signatures.**

Signatures, or **sigs**, are lines of text automatically added after each of our forum posts. They are similar to email signatures.

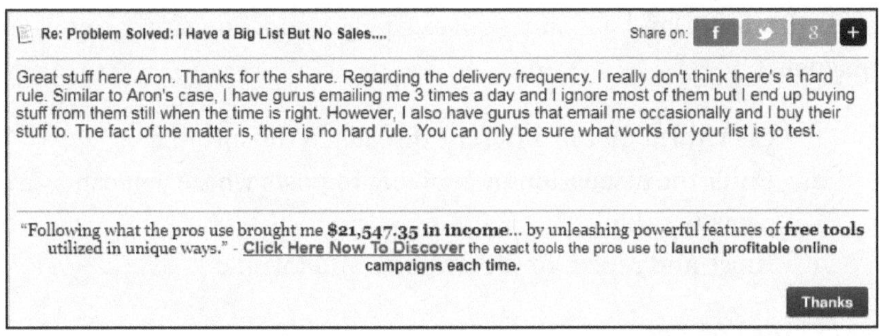

In forums, it's an accepted practice for the signature area to include self-promotional statements with a link or two. Each forum will have its own rules on signatures though, and we need to abide by those rules.

1. Visit each forum on your list.
2. Click on some random posts from several different forum users.
3. Check if the posts have signatures. It's also important to check if those signatures have links to outside sources (i.e., other websites).
4. Sign up for an account on the qualified niche forums.

5. Log in and go to your account settings.
6. Enter your profile details accordingly.
7. Go to the *Signature* settings.
8. Enter the **lead magnet benefit statement** as your signature and include a call to action link to your squeeze page. Doing so entices the forum members to visit our website and download our lead magnet.

Step 3: Participate consistently in the forums

After signing up for an account and setting our signature, it's time to engage with the community.

The idea is to be very helpful and encouraging by answering questions from members who have concerns and providing encouragement for members who are struggling.

As we contribute to the community, our signature appears with each of our posts. Members of the community who are interested can click the link, land on our squeeze page, and download our lead magnet.

1. Click through the different threads in the forum.
2. Enter the discussion by replying to posts where you can provide value.
3. Rinse and repeat for other posts and forums.

<u>Notes for this section</u>

- Google search results are not perfect. The onus of sifting through the search results and filtering the quality niche forums rests on our shoulders.
- As for your account settings, there are many automated and fake accounts online. So it's a good idea to enter your real professional details and add a photo to show the community that you are a real person, not a bot. Credibility goes a long way when building an audience.
- Some forums have signature settings deactivated for <u>new</u> users. In these cases, there are conditions you have to meet before your signature settings go live. Most of the time, you

have to meet a set number of posts and have been a member of the forum for a set length of time. You can see these conditions in the forum's guidelines section. Fulfill these conditions to enable your signature.

- The effectiveness of this method is dependent on consistency. We need to keep on participating at a consistent pace. Eventually, we will develop influence in the community and be able to attract more traffic to our website in the process.

Seed traffic method 3: Reddit participation

Reddit is a social news aggregation website. Members post their thoughts or submit links to news and articles from other sites to share with the community. These submissions appear inside sub-communities called **subreddits**. This keeps the topics organized and easy to find.

Every post (i.e., links and comments) can receive *upvotes* or *downvotes* from other community members. This democratic voting system allows the worthwhile topics to trend, get hot, and rise above the noise and bogus submissions.

Reddit seems like any other forum, bookmarking, social media, online group, or news aggregation website. However, the power of Reddit comes from its highly active, intelligent, and passionate user base. We'll encounter meaningful, witty, and often hilarious discussions from real people here.

For our purposes, interaction with real people is exactly what we need to grow our audience. We'll deal with fewer spambots, fake accounts, and lurkers on our way to building our audience.

1. Visit https://www.reddit.com/.
2. Sign up for an account. Use a creative and cool nickname.
3. Search for active subreddits that are relevant to your niche topic. Go to ***Metareddit*** (http://www.metareddit.com/) for a more powerful and organized subreddit search.
4. Subscribe to at least **three** active and relevant subreddits.

5. For each subreddit that you join, check out the top performing posts by sorting via *Top* instead of *Hot*. Adjust the time frame as necessary. Top-performing posts from the *past month* are a good sweet spot.
6. Once you know what types of posts normally do well in your chosen subreddit, create posts that follow similar compositions.
7. Weave your lead magnet topic into your posts and include a link to your squeeze page where appropriate.
8. Monitor your Reddit post after publishing so you can answer reader comments and inquiries.
9. Rinse and repeat for other posts and subreddits.

Notes for this section

- Cool usernames do better than real usernames in Reddit. There's no need to use your real or pen name as your username here.
- Each subreddit has its guidelines. Read and follow them carefully.
- Don't go against the tide. Emulate top performing posts on the subreddit. Although intelligent, Reddit users (or **redditors**) are prone to "groupthink" – community members do react harshly to opposing views and bury opposing stories with an avalanche of *downvotes*.
- Create quality content. Don't just share links you found on other websites. Share your thoughts and dive into details.
- Don't submit links leading to your website directly. Create posts and weave your link inside the text area whenever relevant.
- If you have a compelling story, unique situation, or above-average accomplishment, you can do an **AMA (Ask Me Anything)** post in a relevant subreddit. These types of posts do well in Reddit.
- Reply to comments on your posts promptly. This will help build momentum and keep your posts on top for much longer.

- Participate regularly. Once a day participation is a good frequency to aim for.

Seed traffic method 4: Quora participation

Quora is a question-and-answer website. In fact, it's one of the most popular. It's a community for asking questions where other members give answers, share advice, and display their expertise for free. Great answers are *upvoted*, raised to the top, and get noticed.

The key audience-building aspect about Quora is it shows the names and credentials of the questions' respondents. This is unique, as other question-and-answer sites only show usernames. The most helpful experts receive badges and appear prominently across the website, leading to more exposure.

For our purposes, Quora is a powerful traffic generation method because it allows us to build our credibility based on our knowledge and expertise. We don't have to know someone. We don't have to have a compelling story. We don't even need a big budget. This gives us a fighting chance of getting noticed and building credibility – as long as we provide useful answers to popular questions.

Since our photo, name, and credentials appear on each question we answer, Quora offers us a powerful way to raise awareness for our brand. Answering specific questions also attracts other people with the same issues, allowing us to build an audience with similar profiles.

1. Visit https://www.quora.com/.
2. Sign up for an account. Choose your topics of interest.
3. Fill up your profile completely. Add a photo, fill up your credentials, and write your story in the *description about yourself* section.
4. Within your description, include the lead magnet benefit statement with a link to your squeeze page.
5. Search for your niche topics' most popular questions. Type your niche topic in Quora's search bar. Look for relevant search suggestions that are prefixed with **Topic:**. Clicking on these results would take you to that topic's own *topic page*. If

the topic is big enough, it would have a *Topic FAQ* tab that you can click on. This would show you all the popular questions on that topic.

6. Answer those popular questions in detail. Weave your lead magnet into the conversation if possible and include a link to your squeeze page.

Notes for this section

- Use your real or pen name in Quora. The real identities of real experts with real credentials are valued here.

- Answer a question at least once a day. Quora has a way of rewarding badges and building your credentials as you become more helpful to the community.

- Aside from questions we can find in the *Topic FAQ* section of a topic, answering questions that have many *follows* can gain amazing traction.

- Deep and detailed answers perform well and get *upvoted* the most. It is best to take the time to consider and compose our answers well.

- Use formatting and images to make our answers stand out visually. Bullet points, boldface text, underscores, block quotes, and white spaces coupled with images can go a long way toward making our answer pop out. These elements also make our answers easier to read.

- Tag the big contributors (i.e., other experts who answer many questions in Quora) to your topic of discussion when applicable. When answering questions, we can type @ and search for the name of the contributors to tag them.

Seed traffic method 5: HARO

HARO stands for "Help A Reporter Out." As the name suggests, the website facilitates a connection between journalists and information sources.

Journalists look for experts and resource persons they can interview to add credibility to their articles. HARO makes it easier and faster for journalists to find expert resource people to quote by connecting members of the working press with a network of subject matter experts and influencers across a wide range of topics.

Being a **resource person** on HARO provides us with opportunities to be interviewed and quoted by journalists who use this resource.

Also, we get the chance to have our names and expertise showcased inside the stories these journalists send to their media organizations. That gives us exposure across the readers these media outfits reach.

We can also add these media exposures to our credentials down the line. Working with journalists of major publications can do miracles for our business that are otherwise impossible using other means.

1. Visit https://www.helpareporter.com/.
2. Sign up as a *source*.
3. Fill in the necessary details. The email address is particularly important.
4. Check your relevant topics of expertise in the HARO *preferences* section.
5. Receive source requests daily in your email address and look through them.
6. If you qualify for the requirements of a source request, send out a pitch.
7. Wait for the journalist to reach out to you. Discuss how to move forward from there.

Notes for this section

- Read the journalist's source request carefully and respond with complete information. This will increase your chances of getting a favorable response.
- Be professional.
- Check your HARO newsletter regularly.
- If you fit the requirements of a journalist, pitch <u>immediately</u>. Most of these journalists are on a tight deadline.

- Only choose specific industries that you are competent in. Don't select *Master HARO*. Source requests go to specific sources first before they funnel out to the *Master HARO* sources.
- Always tread carefully with interviews that may involve exchanges – offered due to generosity (like tokens of appreciation) or necessity (like product samples for review) – on either side. Integrity is the currency of any business, so make sure that these material contributions don't influence or skew the outcome in any way.

Seed traffic method 6: Influencer outreach

Influencer outreach is the process of connecting with the influencers in your niche. The purpose is to initiate a win-win exchange. We make the influencer an irresistible offer that can improve their business and bottom line. In exchange, we receive an opportunity to work with the influencer – or, at the very least, gain an exposure to their audience base.

Influencer outreach is one of the most powerful forms of marketing and traffic generation. It exposes our business to a mass audience from the get-go. It also gives us credibility by association. Successfully getting a big name influencer to feature us or talk about our business catapults our expert status in the industry on the spot.

We refer to the **niche influencers** document that we created during our research phase to jumpstart our influencer outreach campaign. The traffic data serves as a good measure of how popular these influencers are.

Now that we have an initial list of influencers to reach out to, it's time to determine what value we can offer, get the influencer's email address, and send a value pitch.

Step 1: Determine the value we can offer

Before we can get on an influencer's radar, we need to offer them value. The perception of value is subjective, but influencers do find at least one of the following offers valuable.

- **Offer 1: Free valuable favor**. Influencers pay attention if you offer to implement a favor that can concretely benefit their business. This can range from implementing better business strategies for the influencer to connecting the influencer with another relevant influencer whom you know for possible business partnerships.
The success of this offer hinges on the fact that the results you can provide must be concrete and measurable. Also, keep in mind that your contribution should be specific to the influencer's business, not just a generic sales pitch.

    1. Research the influencer's business or website.
    2. Determine what service you can offer to improve it.
    3. Reach out to the influencer and make your value pitch.

- **Offer 2: Unsolicited testimonials.** If the influencer has a product that you've used before, reach out and share your results from using that product. Any influencer would welcome positive feedback about his or her product. Provide as much practical proof as you can. Show observable results like "before and after" pictures of you losing X lbs. thanks to their weight loss program or product. Business reports showing a sales increase of X percent from using a product works great as well. You get the idea.

    1. Check the products you have purchased in the past six months that are relevant to your niche.
    2. Document the results you have achieved by using those products.
    3. Reach out to the influencers behind each of those products.

- **Offer 3: Proven content.** Offering an article for publishing on an influencer's blog is known as **guest posting**. Influencers love any content that can give them more page views and website hits, regardless of who writes them.

The topic of your pitch article should be relevant to the influencer's blog and audience. Pitch the article idea before actually writing the article. This saves you time if the idea gets rejected or needs more refinement. To increase the chances of success, provide references that prove articles similar to your pitch article have gone viral.

1. Figure out if the influencer has accepted **guest posts** in the past. Check their recent blog posts to see if they have published articles written by other authors.
2. Determine the subject matter of the influencer's blog. What main topics does the blog cover?
3. Perform searches for your influencer's blog topics on https://app.buzzsumo.com/ by using the **content research** tool of Buzzsumo.
4. Take note of the articles with lots of *shares* and have gone viral. These article topics are worth pitching to your influencer. You also have historical proof as a reference that your article topic idea would work.
5. Reach out to the influencer.

Step 2: Get the influencer's email address

The best way to reach out to an influencer is through email. We can contact influencers through their social media pages, but there's a high chance that our message will not reach the influencer via this route. Many influencers don't check their social media pages regularly. Some influencers even hire social media specialists to manage their social media pages and accounts. Any fan can reach out to influencers via social media also, so our pitch can easily get buried beneath the noise along those avenues.

On the flip side, everyone still checks their personal email inboxes themselves. People simply don't pass off the management of their email accounts to other people.

There are several ways to get hold of an influencer's email address.

- **Option 1: Influencer's website.** The most direct approach to get an influencer's email address, short of asking them for it directly, is to go to their website. Look for the email addresses listed on the *Contact Us* or *About Us* pages. At the very least, you'll encounter a contact form through which you can reach the influencer. You can also find and use the email address at the bottom of the *privacy policy* page of the influencer's website in some cases.
- **Option 2: Hunter.io.** *Hunter.io* (formerly known as *Email Hunter*) is an online service that facilitates email address search and verification, especially those that aren't freely posted in public.

  1. Visit https://www.hunter.io/.
  2. Sign up for a free account. A free account grants 100 search credits per month. This is more than enough for our purposes at this stage.
  3. Type the website domain of the influencer.
  4. Find the name of the influencer from the results and take note of the email address.

Step 3: Email a pitch

A winning pitch is half the battle. The pitch gets your foot through the influencer's door. There is no "magic bullet" formula that works for everyone. A compelling *subject line* and a short-and-to-the-point message, however, can increase our likelihood of success.

Here's how all the components of the pitch come together.

- **Component 1: Subject line.** Remember the emphasis on measurable results for all of the value offers from Step 1? It works well to use concrete outcomes in the *subject line* of your email as well. Here are example results-oriented subject lines.

o   *I used <name of influencer's product> and got <results you achieved>, here's what happened...*

o   *751 shares and 45 comments. Interested?* (tip: we can approximate potential shares and comments stats using **Buzzsumo** research on articles similar to what we are pitching)

- **Component 2: Pitch body.** It's best to keep the pitch direct to the point. Influencers are busy people who don't have the time to read a long email. A good structure to follow is *rapport* ➔ *offer* ➔ *proof* ➔ *call to action.*

  1. **Rapport.** Begin with a greeting and a story about how you got to know the influencer. This builds rapport. You can say that you are a longtime reader of his blog. You can tell the influencer how she inspired you at a conference. Keep it honest and simple.

  2. **Offer.** After the introduction, go straight to the offer – tell the influencer your reason for emailing him/her. You can explain the favor you intend to do for them. You can say you're using their product and express how it benefited you. You can ask if they are interested in a guest post (include the title idea/proposed headline for your article).

  3. **Proof.** Immediately follow that up with proof of the promise you made in the subject line. Provide screenshots, links, and references as proof of your claims.

  4. **Call to action.** End the pitch with a call to action. The idea is to keep the conversation going and moving forward. At the very least, invite them to reply to your email and discuss next steps or ask questions. Open up communication lines through which they may respond to you.

When our pitch gets accepted, we engage in discussions leading to fulfilling our promises. In the end, we are hoping that kindness will beget kindness (i.e., helping the influencer will trigger their generosity to help us in return). The influencer may be inclined to propose a business deal with us, open us to their audience, or allow a link to our squeeze page inside our guest post.

Notes for this section

- When offering your services, make sure to focus more on pitching the measurable results and what you want to do for the influencer vs. explaining who you are and what you do as a profession.

- When offering unsolicited testimonials, it's not enough to write a paragraph raving about the influencer's product — this is overdone. Stand out by detailing your entire experience of using their product, backing it up with proof of your positive outcome.

- When offering guest posts, never copy or plagiarize. Use Buzzsumo only as a benchmark for well-performing articles. Improve on the points provided by those articles for your pitch to the influencer.

- If your guest post is accepted, monitor your post for two days after it's published. It will help you and your business if you can respond to the post readers' comments and inquiries.

- When getting the influencer's email address, avoid role-based email addresses. Role-based email addresses are addresses like admin@influencerdomain.com, info @influencerdomain.com, newsletter@influencerdomain .com, or the very forthright no-reply@influencerdomain .com. These role-based email addresses facilitate certain functions of the business and are not checked regularly. Find other, more personal, email addresses through which to contact the influencer.

- There is no tool that can provide 100% accuracy. However, when it comes to email address search and verification, Hunter.io comes close.

- Signing up for a free account on Hunter.io requires a business email address – webmail services like ***Gmail*** and ***Yahoo! Mail*** are not accepted. This won't be a problem since we purchased our own domain – we can easily create a custom business email address like **yourpenname@your domain.com**.

- A key Hunter.io feature is that it extracts data from multiple sources to verify the validity of the email addresses. Hover your cursor over the circle beside the email addresses you want to check to see the *confidence score*. The *confidence score* shows the reliability of the email address. Clicking on the *check mark* verifies that the email address is active and doesn't bounce.

- Influencer outreach is a delicate proposition. Don't expect every influencer you contact to respond positively – or at all – to you. However, just one endorsement from a popular influencer can give your business an instant boost, so take time to fine-tune your pitch.

Traffic Generation: Wrap-Up and Pro Tips

Traffic is the fuel that keeps the entire Agile Online Income Machine running. Without traffic, our Online Marketing machine practically does not exist – because it can't fulfill its intended purpose.

As long as we have traffic running through our Agile Online Income Machine, we have a shot at making money. An imperfect machine can still produce output so long as it's running. A perfect machine that is stagnant can never produce any output. Traffic is king when it comes to Online Marketing.

This chapter shares the most effective traffic generation strategies available for Online Marketers starting from scratch. With minimal money, industry clout, or influencer connections, we need to rely on creativity and grit to jumpstart our online business and attract visitors to our website.

During the infancy of our online business, most of our focus should be on traffic generation, with the intention of building a sizable audience. Once we have a substantial audience base, a lot more traffic generation options will open up to us.

As we go about generating traffic for our website, here are some pro tips to keep in mind.

Tip 1: Follow the community rules

Each existing community we enter for our traffic generation purposes follow a different set of rules. We need to follow them carefully, or it's game over.

Influencers, moderators, admins, and community members are motivated to protect their online havens from spam, bots, and unethical users. Violating any of their rules can get us banned. Therefore, we need to familiarize ourselves with the community's guidelines before making any moves.

Tip 2: Mimic what works

The best way to be successful in any traffic generation is to emulate behavior that has a track record of working. Observe the types of articles that a particular influencer accepts as guest posts, watch which posts get the most shares, benchmark what headlines get the most responses, and mirror the posts that go viral in a community (e.g., AMAs in Reddit). Success leaves clues. Be observant – find them, follow them, and we are likely to get the same results.

Tip 3: Start with two

We discussed several traffic generation methods in this chapter. Intuitively, more traffic sources would logically mean more overall traffic to our website – but the opposite is true. Lack of focus can prevent us from gaining substantial traffic because unpaid traffic sources take time to bear fruit. We need to get involved in the community or build relationships with influencers before we can reap results.

In that sense, it's best to choose two traffic generation methods, master them, and work on getting substantial traffic from these sources. Once we've established our foothold with these traffic generation methods, we can expand to other traffic generation options.

Tip 4: All traffic should lead to downloads

We should always carry the mindset of growing our audience base. This is the only way to ensure the growth of (and consistent earnings for) our online business. Whatever we do online – especially when it comes to generating traffic – should <u>always</u> lead to collecting email addresses and growing our audience.

By executing on our traffic generation methods, we are starting the engine of our Agile Online Income Machine. At this stage, our Online Marketing machine works on building our audience base with qualified email addresses.

Now we need to extend the capabilities of our machine – turning our audience into fans who know, like and trust us. It's time to work on adding the **relationship-building machine** component.

Chapter 7
The "Know, Like, and Trust" Factor

Stage 2 - Relationship-Building Machine

"You don't close a sale; you open a relationship if you want to build a long-term, successful enterprise." – Patricia Fripp

The Road to Income is Paved with Strong Relationships

Any marriage proposal could turn into a disaster and lead to a painfully awkward way home. Although, if one is lucky, the answer to the proposal might be the single greatest word in the English language – yes.

In many ways, our Agile Online Income Machine is like dating. The first step is to get the person's attention and attempt to strike a connection. If all goes well, the pair builds a relationship by give and take, as well as by sharing mutual experiences and bonding activities. When the bond between the couple matures, the perfect time to take that leap of faith arrives – it's time to propose marriage. Hearing a "yes" then paves the way for a "happily ever after" married life.

With our **stage 1: audience-building machine**, we've caught our niche crowd's attention. They visited our website, subscribed to get our lead magnet, and become part of our audience base. Making offers and asking for sales now, as most Online Marketers do, is a risky matter that can work only in the rarest of instances. We are more likely to have rejection slapped on our faces. Similar to dating, proposing too soon can lead to rejection.

People only do business with people they know, like, and trust. Our audience only knows a bit about us. We haven't given enough basis for our audience to like us yet. We surely haven't proven ourselves worthy of our audience's trust.

It's time to build that relationship before "getting down on one knee" and asking for the sale.

The Two Types of Emails: Broadcast vs. Sequence

We use our email marketing app to build and work on our relationship-building machine. We are already familiar with the email marketing app's ability to collect email addresses. This basic functionality involves creating forms that we embed in our website, where visitors can then enter their contact information to subscribe.

Now, we need to dive into another one of our email marketing app's core functionalities – sending emails. Every email marketing app can send out two types of emails – **broadcast emails** and **sequence emails**. We can choose to send the emails we write to our audience as a broadcast, or as part of a sequence. Let us understand the difference.

Type 1: Broadcast Emails

Broadcast emails are emails that we write and send to our audience (or a segment of our audience) if we want them to receive our emails at the same time. This works like sending a one-off email and *cc'ing* all the intended recipients. We can also write the email and broadcast it at a future schedule. The idea is that all the intended recipients receive that email at the same time.

Broadcast emails, being a one-off, are best for announcing time-sensitive news and finite product offers.

Type 2: Sequence emails

Sequence emails, otherwise known as **follow-up emails** or **autoresponder emails**, are emails that we write and set up to send automatically right after a trigger event. This trigger event is typically the moment the visitor subscribes using the opt-in form.

We chain together multiple sequence emails to form an **email series**, also known as a **follow-up series** or **autoresponder sequence**. The emails in the series are sent one after the other at set time intervals (called a **drip schedule**) between emails. The email series will then run continuously as long as there are still sequence emails scheduled within that series.

The moment of request or trigger event is important. Unlike **broadcast emails**, our audience doesn't receive each email at the same time, only in the same order. Our audience receives emails based on the time they subscribed and entered the email series.

Refer to the illustration below for a clearer contrast.

Since sequence emails can be set to send emails to audiences automatically, they are best for automated relationship-building purposes with our audience.

Notes for this section

- *Mailchimp* uses the term **campaigns** to refer to sending emails, among other things. They also use **regular campaigns** for broadcast emails and **automated campaigns/workflows** for creating an email series (you can then load sequence emails within that automated campaign/workflow). Both of these can be found and created by going to *Campaigns* ➜ *Create Campaign* ➜ *Create an Email*, then clicking on *Regular* or *Automated* depending on what you want to create.

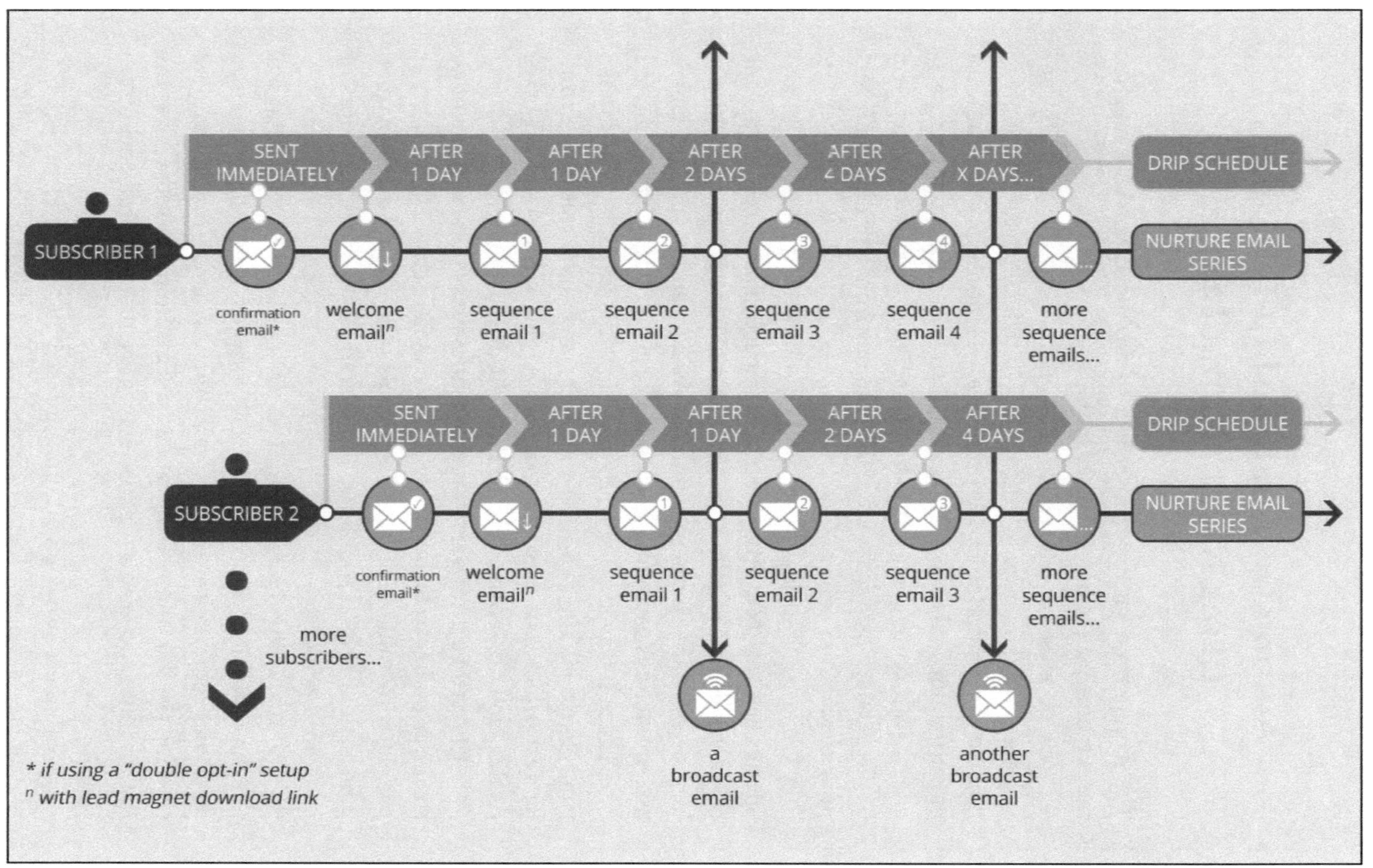
SUBSCRIBER 1
SENT IMMEDIATELY
AFTER 1 DAY
AFTER 1 DAY
AFTER 2 DAYS
AFTER 4 DAYS
AFTER X DAYS...
DRIP SCHEDULE
NURTURE EMAIL SERIES
confirmation email*
welcome email^n
sequence email 1
sequence email 2
sequence email 3
sequence email 4
more sequence emails...
SUBSCRIBER 2
SENT IMMEDIATELY
AFTER 1 DAY
AFTER 1 DAY
AFTER 2 DAYS
AFTER 4 DAYS
DRIP SCHEDULE
NURTURE EMAIL SERIES
confirmation email*
welcome email^n
sequence email 1
sequence email 2
sequence email 3
more sequence emails...
more subscribers...
a broadcast email
another broadcast email
* if using a "double opt-in" setup
^{n} with lead magnet download link

Automatic Relationship-Building: Using Nurture Email Series

The moment our visitors subscribed to download our lead magnet, they became part of our audience base.

We've already established that initial connection with our audience. We then need to nurture this initial connection carefully to become an enduring and profitable relationship. The aim of nurturing our audience is to get them to know, like, and trust us – and convert our audience into our fans. Fans, nurtured into a warm business relationship, are more likely to buy from us rather than cold prospects.

While online marketers follow different philosophies and approaches to converting their audience base into fans, the consensus is that relationship with the audience grows cold with the lack of constant communication. Likewise, sending useless emails and promotions can make your audience give you the cold shoulder.

The best way to build a relationship with our audience is to send <u>valuable</u> emails <u>constantly</u>. We do so by creating a **nurture email series**, which has two components – the **agile email series** method and the **frontloaded drip schedule** technique.

The **agile email series** method guarantees that every email we send our audience through our nurture email series is perceived as packed with value. Our valuable emails make us a source of good information, helpful solutions, and overall positive feelings from our audience's perspective.

All the while, the **frontloaded drip schedule** technique sets the schedule for our nurture email series. This allows enough constant communication to keep the audience warm without crossing the line and making us an irritant. Doing so keeps us at the top of our audience's minds and prevents our audience from forgetting us.

With these two configurations infused into our sequence emails, we can create a nurture email series that provides constant value to our audience on autopilot – a powerful "set-it-and-forget-it" relationship-building machine.

Write value emails always: Using the Agile Email Series method

The nurture email series needs to be pre-loaded with emails of value to our audience. Our email marketing app can't send any emails automatically if we don't write emails for it to send out. Also keep in mind, if we send junk email to our audience, even once, we'll lose a whole chunk of it through *unsubscribes.*

Here is where it gets tricky. There are many schools of thought from different Online Marketing experts about creating your email series. Most experts teach that you need to pre-load one month's worth of sequence emails into the email series, at three to four emails sent weekly, before launching. That requires us to write 12 to 16 emails and load them into our email marketing app <u>before</u> we launch our campaign and let subscribers in. We must then keep adding more emails post-launch to lengthen the email series indefinitely.

When I was starting, I followed this advice. However, it soon dawned on me that this way of building an email series is a risky hit-or-miss affair. Value is relative – what we as marketers find valuable may not be what our future audience will find valuable. So pre-writing one month's worth of emails before getting our first subscriber in is like shooting in the dark.

I found a different approach to writing our initial email series that doesn't require risking valuable time planning and writing multiple emails from the get-go. This approach also guarantees that each email we include in our nurture email series are valuable to our audience. I call it the **agile email series** method.

1. Prepare your **welcome email** if you haven't done so. You are already familiar with this since we covered this in the **Assemble our audience: Using an email marketing app** section in Chapter 5. The welcome email is the first email (the second email, if you enabled double opt-in confirmation) that your audience receives after signing up

for your lead magnet. This contains your welcome message as well as the download instructions for your lead magnet.

2. Write a **trailing question email**. A **trailing question email** asks the subscriber about the biggest obstacle they are facing in the niche, <u>while also</u> being the last email (therefore, trailing) in the entire nurture email series. In one of my niches, my trailing question email looks like this.

****

SUBJECT LINE:
Who else Wants to Earn $4,527.83 in a Month doing Affiliate Marketing?

BODY:
Hey there,

A few months back I have earned $4,527.83 in a
single month doing Affiliate Marketing.

That is when I knew I made it. I have been earning
more since.

It is not a huge deal compared to the top affiliates
who earn tens of thousands of dollars each month.

But it was a big deal for me, considering that I failed
my first four years of Internet Marketing – tanking 17
different websites in the process.

I have overcome the same struggles, frustrations, and
disappointments that you may be facing right now.

I've solved problems, discovered solutions, and figured
out what works in Affiliate Marketing that would get you
over the hump.

If you are having trouble, let me help you.

Simply take five minutes, reply to this email and tell me...

"What is the most frustrating Affiliate Marketing obstacle you facing right now?"

Go ahead. Let me help.

Sincerely,

Kurt Roswell

****

It doesn't have to be that long. The main component is that question at the very end. This question will encourage your audience to share their most pressing issues and problems. Their replies will form the basis of your other emails in the nurture email series.

3. Add the trailing question email to send after the welcome email in the email series. You do this by adding a sequence email within the appropriate campaign. Select the campaign where you created your welcome email. Click on *Add Email* to add an email to this email series. Don't mind the *Edit trigger* for now. We'll discuss the time intervals between emails on the next section when we get to drip schedules.

4. At this point, our nurture email series only runs like *welcome email* ➜ *trailing question email*. When an audience replies with a concern or question, create a sequence email addressing that concern or question. The principle is that we always use our audience as the basis of what we write and serve them, not our own intuition filled with biases.

5. Insert that new sequence email into the nurture email series and move the trailing question email to the tail of the series. This makes our nurture email series look like *welcome email → sequence email 1 (answers an audience question) → trailing question email.* Edit the trailing question email as necessary so it makes sense along the nurture email series, since some of your audience already saw it when they first signed up.

6. Repeat and keep growing the nurture email series as more concerns and questions come from your audience. As an illustration, your nurture email series will grow like this.

   o *welcome email → trailing question email*

   o *welcome email → sequence email 1 (answers an audience question) → trailing question email*

   o *welcome email → sequence email 1 (answers an audience question) → sequence email 2 (answers another audience question) → trailing question email*

   o *welcome email → sequence email 1 (answers an audience question) → sequence email 2 (answers another audience question) → sequence email 3 (answers a different audience question) → trailing question email*

   o *And so on...*

The agile email series method allows us to keep growing our nurture email series with only valuable emails included since the basis came from our audience themselves. This maximizes our relationship-building machine's proficiency in turning our audience into fans each step of the way.

It's called the agile email series method because it adjusts on the fly and allows us to co-create our nurture email series with our audience. This is the most effective and efficient way to build an email series from scratch.

Notes for this section

- At the start, our nurture email series only goes like *welcome email → trailing question email*. Once the trailing question email gets sent, the subscriber has reached the end of the nurture email series and no more follow-ups after that. We still need to keep the relationship warm by sending out emails and keeping in constant contact though. To solve this, we can send industry updates or refer valuable articles to our audience using broadcast emails while we are still building our nurture email series. Once we've loaded more sequence emails to answer the replies we got from our trailing question email, we can start lowering the frequency for sending broadcast emails about industry updates and articles to our audience. The nurture email series will start to take over our relationship-building automatically.

Keep our audience warm: Using the Frontloaded Drip schedule

Now that we already know what email topics to write about, there's that matter of deciding on the frequency of our emails.

Knowing how often we should send emails to our audience is as important as knowing what to write about. Send too many emails, and our audience will view us as a nuisance, and they may unsubscribe. Send too few, and they'll forget about us. Both scenarios don't help with relationship-building and are detrimental to turning our audience into fans.

The timetable for sending emails that is followed by an email series is called a **drip schedule**. We set up this drip schedule by editing the interval or delay between each sequence email in our email series.

By configuring the drip schedule of our nurture email series, we control how frequently our audience gets an email follow-up from us – starting from the time they subscribed and received our welcome email. We can set our audience to receive an email X days after the welcome email, then another email Y days after that, then another email Z days after that, and so on.

Now, when it comes to setting up the best drip schedule, let me share an important email marketing principle with you – the audience is warmest at the moment after they subscribe. Our audience has peak awareness and interest in our brand immediately after they've downloaded our lead magnet. This is also the point when our audience is most receptive to our messages. As time passes, the excitement wanes, and the audience slowly shifts their attention to other matters.

Knowing this principle, the most effective way to configure a drip schedule is by having frequent emails at the start of the nurture email series and lessening the frequency later on. This approach maximizes the excitement of the audience after subscription. Lessening the frequency along the way allows us to keep constant contact with our audience without turning into an annoyance. This is the **frontloaded drip schedule** technique.

With the **frontloaded drip schedule**, our audience should receive an email from us every day for the next six days after subscribing. We then slowly transition to one email <u>every other day</u> for the following week. On the third week onwards, we transition to one email and skipping two days. The frontloaded drip schedule would make our nurture email series flow like this.

Week 1 and 2:	*W-E-E-E-E-E / E-0-E-0-E-0-E /*
Week 3, 4, 5, and repeat onwards:	*0-0-E-0-0-E-0 / 0-E-0-0-E-0-0 / E-0-0-E-0-0-E / …*

LEGEND: *W = welcome email, E = sequence email, 0 = skip day*

Scheduling the value-laden sequence emails for our nurture email series this way maximizes our interaction and relationship-building with our audience.

Anatomy of Powerful Emails

Writing emails is just like writing articles or blog posts, except emails are shorter and more personal. The intent of any email, especially the sequence emails that comprise our nurture email series, is to entice our recipients to open our email, read, and perform a **call to action**. This call to action can be a reply to our email, a click on a link to read an article, follow our social media pages, or check out and buy an offer.

We have already established the mechanism for receiving inquiries in the previous section. The agile email series method will constantly feed us with topic ideas for our writing.

Now, it's time to write those emails. We can write an email any way we like. If you are having a hard time writing your sequence emails, here's a structure that you can use as a guide to make the process easier – *subject line* ➔ *hook intro* ➔ *main body* ➔ *call to action* ➔ *signature* ➔ *P.S. line* ➔ *business address + unsubscribe button.*

Element 1: Subject line

For most people, the **subject line** only refers to the title of the email. It's beneficial to look at the subject line as the entire line appearing in the recipient's email inbox. This **extended subject line** includes the **from** field, **email title**, **email snippet**, and the **timestamp**.

This line, with all these elements, is what our audience sees. Our audience scans this entire subject line and makes a split-second decision to either open or ignore our email. This is your one shot.

Make sure your brand (i.e., your pen name) appears on the **from** field correctly. Use an accurate but curiosity-inducing headline, and draw interest with the **email snippet**. The email snippet shows the first few words of the email content.

Element 2: Hook intro

We start an email with a **hook intro** to lure the reader into the email and entice them to read the rest of the email text. Starting this way also leverages the fact that the first few words of our hook intro appear as the email snippet in the subject line. This approach, then, gives us twice the luring power. For effective hook intros, start your emails with captivating stories or powerful benefits. What would the reader achieve if they read the rest of the email and follow its instructions?

Element 3: Main body

The **main body** is the part where we tell our audience the reason why we are emailing them. It's in the main body that we show the solution to the problem or the bulk of our message.

Element 4: Call to action

Emails aren't just meant to be read. We, as marketers, should keep the conversation going. We use **calls to action** to lead our audience to the next step, while also making it a habit for our audience to perform the actions we put in front of them. These actions usually involve clicking on a link to something valuable. Leading our audience to actions that are beneficial to them is an exercise to build trust and move the relationship forward.

At the very least, we should invite our audience to reply to our emails with their questions, or ask for feedback. Doing this encourages interaction between our audience and us.

Element 5: Signature

It's always good to remind our audience whom the emails come from. Wrap the email up with a simple salutation and your name or pen name. You can also include links to your social media pages in the **signature**.

Element 6: P.S. line

The **P.S. (postscript)** line includes any afterthoughts we wish to add to our email. There's an interesting phenomenon though – the "P.S." is the most read part of an email, aside from the subject line. For whatever reason, human brains seem wired to read P.S. statements. It's wise to take advantage of this phenomenon. The P.S. line is best for reiterating our call to action.

Element 7: Business address + unsubscribe button

Every business email and subscription is required, by law, to include the **sender's business address** and an **unsubscribe button**. Email marketing apps adopted this rule, and will automatically include these components in every email we send.

<u>Notes for this section</u>

- Put a gap <u>between</u> the **main email** and the **business address + unsubscribe button**. The two latter elements are mandatory components put in place by email marketing apps. Functionally, we can't remove them. Legally, we shouldn't remove them. So those components are there to stay. Now, every time our audience sees that unsubscribe button, it gives them a subconscious suggestion or inclination to do just that. We want our audience to have the freedom to unsubscribe – it is their right, after all. However, we don't want to tempt them to unsubscribe for no good reason. Therefore, it's a great idea to put a gap between our main email and the unsubscribe button. Simply put 10 to 15 lines (by pressing the *enter* or *return* key) between the main email and the unsubscribe button. This sends the unsubscribe button to the periphery and prevents unintentional unsubscribes.

Stage 2 - Relationship-Building Machine: Wrap-Up and Pro Tips

People only do business with people they know, like, and trust. That marketing adage has held true for the longest time. Asking for a sale without first establishing a "know, like, and trust" relationship with the audience will result in apathy and rejection. It's important to turn our audience into fans so they will be more receptive to our offers later on. We build this relationship by engaging with our audience in a continuous dialogue using valuable and consistent emails.

After going through this chapter, we should have started evolving our audience-building machine into a relationship-building machine. We should have the makings of an automated series of valuable emails sent to our audience consistently.

Through a chain of sequence emails, we build a nurture email series that serves our audience, builds relationships, turns them into fans, and keeps us at the top of their minds, all on autopilot. This can be supplemented further with valuable broadcast emails when necessary.

The key element here is value. Always provide value. <u>Never,</u> ever, think about spamming the audience.

Here are some pro tips to enhance our relationship-building effectiveness.

Tip 1: Short emails over long emails

Keep emails short and get straight to the point or they won't get read. People go through their emails in batches – opening their inboxes and scanning serially through multiple emails in a single sitting. Long emails are intimidating to look at and will get ignored.

If we can't fit all our valuable information inside a single short email, we can remedy the situation in one of two ways. First, publish the information as a blog post, then use the email as a teaser that includes a link to that blog post. Second, we can break the long, valuable set of information into several emails and send them as a mini-series.

In general, sending any email that spans 400 words or more is flirting with the patience of your readers.

Tip 2: Set the proper email width

Emails that are too wide are also intimidating and tiring to read. Worse, if the screen is small – like those of tablets and mobile phones – the audience will be reading the email using a horizontal scroll bar. The constant scrolling back and forth creates unnecessary difficulty for our audience.

Let's keep our emails at 550 to 600 pixels wide. Or, to make things simpler, keep a 65-character maximum for each line.

Tip 3: Email to promote updates

Whether we have new blog articles, published guest posts, media appearances, business appearances, or business developments, remember to email our audience about these new developments. Let's be proactive and update our audience via email using a broadcast or sequence email. Use whichever approach applies to the situation.

Now that we have extended our Agile Online Income Machine to include the functions necessary for automated relationship-building, it's time to start thinking of monetization. We are turning our audience into fans, we can start establishing a win-win exchange of selling premium solutions in exchange for money.

Chapter 8
Reaping What We Sow

Stage 3 - Passive Income Machine

"If you don't find a way to make money while you sleep, you will work until you die." – Warren Buffet

Show Me the Money!

"Show me the money!" Jerry yells as he makes a fool of himself inside his office, trying to convince one of his clients to keep him on as his sports agent. He succeeds as Rod, his football player client, replies with "Congratulations. You're still my agent."

This is an iconic scene from the critically acclaimed and commercially successful 1996 romantic comedy-drama sports film **Jerry Maguire**. It's a great movie that gave us some of the cheesiest, but "right in the feels" one-liners like "you complete me" and "you had me at hello."

After getting our audience with our "hello," we move on to completing the relationship – in our endeavor, this means making money by providing genuinely valuable products.

The perfect time to start considering monetization for our online business is when we've reached an audience size of 450 to 500 subscribers. The immediate reason is that the price of most email marketing app increases at the 501 audience-size mark. Making sales before hitting the 501 mark allows us to absorb any increase in cost while still making a profit.

A more important reason for waiting to grow to an audience size of 450 to 500 before considering monetization is that, at that size, we now have a reliable source for monetization ideas. We can ask our audience about their wants and needs, and then sell the perfect solutions to help them. If we do the work and offer the products that best fit our audience, making sales and earning money becomes easier.

We've already projected a great first impression with our audience-building machine. We've followed up on that positive impression by providing genuine value using our relationship-building machine.

Now, our audience of fans already "know, like, and trust" us. It's the proper time to evolve our Agile Online Income Machine to a **passive income machine** by adding the monetization component. This "completes the relationship."

When it comes to offering solutions to our audience, it's fun and rewarding, both emotionally and financially, to be able to sell our own products. It is more prudent, however, to sell other people's products first – an approach called **affiliate marketing**.

Sell Other People's Products: Be an Affiliate

An **affiliate**, or **affiliate seller**, is an individual who earns a commission from selling other peoples' (merchant) products or services. The term **affiliate** is used online in the same way as the term **agent** is used offline.

As an affiliate, we have no employee-employer relationship with the merchant. Nor are we involved in their business operations. Our association with the merchant is limited to selling their products and receiving a commission for each sale we make, or whatever terms we've agreed upon.

It's a great move to monetize (earn money) with our Agile Online Income Machine as an affiliate before going to other monetization models. Starting out as an affiliate allows us to make money immediately by selling products that are already available in the market.

This allows us to cover the expenses for running our Agile Online Income Machine while we are growing our audience base and, possibly, give us extra income for tools and outsourcing.

Starting out as an affiliate saves us the expensive and stressful ordeal of dealing with customer service as well. Merchants are the responsible party for handling customer issues and complaints.

The most important advantage of starting out as an affiliate though, is that it allows us to test the market response of our audience before we set out creating a product of our own. This reduces our risk of investing valuable resources in creating a product that may end up failing. We can also develop products with a much deeper sense of what our audience wants.

Let's discuss how to get started as an affiliate.

Step 1: Apply for affiliate products

Merchants run **affiliate programs** to extend the reach of their products or services beyond their own audience. This is their way of getting more sales. Merchants then run **affiliate marketing apps** to facilitate the acceptance, tracking, reporting, and payment of affiliates who sell their products and services.

In general, we can get into an affiliate relationship with a merchant depending on how they run their affiliate programs. There are **affiliate networks**, **independent affiliate programs**, and **exclusive affiliate programs**.

- **Program 1: Affiliate networks. Affiliate networks** are platforms that serve as a marketplace for merchants and affiliates. Merchants put their products up for sale in the affiliate network. Affiliates can then choose from an assortment of products from different merchants to sell. The affiliate network acts as the central hub running all the transactions and processes between the merchants and the sellers (i.e., crediting sales, releasing commissions, providing reports).
  We can sign up with affiliate networks, search for products

that are applicable to our audience, get our **affiliate link**, and start promoting the products we choose to our fans. Here is a list of the most popular affiliate networks to get you started.

- o **ClickBank** - https://www.clickbank.com/
- o **CJ Affiliate** (formerly **Commission Junction**) - http://www.cj.com/
- o **ShareASale** - https://www.shareasale.com/
- o **JVZoo** - https://www.jvzoo.com/
- o **Amazon Associates** - https://affiliate-program .amazon.com/

- **Program 2: Independent affiliate program.** If you already know the particular product that you want to sell and it's not listed in any affiliate network, the merchant may be running his own affiliate program. The merchant probably uses his own affiliate marketing app to manage affiliates and facilitate transactions. These are the **independent affiliate programs**.
To apply for **independent affiliate programs**, go to the merchant or product website. You'll normally see a link in the navigation that says *affiliates* – this details the merchant's affiliate acceptance procedure. Follow the application and approval process and you'll be an affiliate seller of their product in no time.
- **Program 3: Exclusive affiliate program.** In the rarest cases, some merchants and product owners run **exclusive affiliate programs**. They don't announce that they accept affiliate sellers to the public. Rather, exclusive affiliate programs only deal with industry elites and thought leaders who have sizable audiences. These affiliate arrangements can pay handsomely. Since there are only a handful of affiliates selling the product, there is less competition. The exclusivity also creates the perception of rarity or privilege for the product. Think of this as similar to having exclusive

distributorship or exclusive licenses in the offline business space.

There is no clear-cut formula for joining an exclusive affiliate program. Most merchants who use exclusive affiliate programs have strong relationships with existing marketers in the niche and only invite these people to become affiliates. The best way to get your foot in the door is to contact the merchant or product owner personally and find out if they are willing to accept you as an affiliate. This is where having a large audience of 25,000 active email addresses or more on your list can open doors for you.

Make a list of **five to ten** relevant solutions in your niche that allow affiliate arrangements.

Step 2: Assess the affiliate products' sales pages

Not all affiliate products or services are good. Only a handful of affiliate solutions are extraordinary. A more sizable number has subpar quality. It's our job to find and select the most fitting products for our audience out of the pool of irrelevant, mediocre, and scammy products flooding the market.

Believe it or not, product quality is only a secondary indicator of how successfully something will sell – and, by extension, how successfully we can offer it to our audience and make money.

The primary factor to consider when it comes to selling affiliate products is the product's sales page – the product's main page, where visitors can see the product image, read the product description and features, and purchase the product.

The sales page acts as the product's digital salesman. Having a good sales page will greatly influence the decision of visitors to purchase the product once you send them to this page.

Product quality ensures client retention and minimal customer service issues. However, our audience won't get to discover the quality of the product if the sales copy can't do its job. Good product quality prevents returns and refunds. The sales page allows us to sell the product in the first place.

Now, assessing a product's sales page is very subjective. Our primary basis for assessment should be the alignment of what's shown and written in the product's sales page vs. what our audience wants.

This is where all of that relationship-building with our audience comes in handy. With the questions and responses that we get from our relationship-building machine, we should have a substantial idea of what resonates with our audience.

Filter your list of affiliate products based on their respective sales pages vs. your understanding of your audience. That is how you determine the best potential products to offer to your audience.

Step 3: Generate the affiliate link

Becoming an affiliate can be a quick sign-up process, or a tedious application procedure, depending on the type of affiliate program the merchant uses. Follow the merchant's instructions to become an affiliate.

Once approved, the first thing we need to do is secure and configure our **affiliate link**. The affiliate link is an actual website link (yes, an ugly piece of URL string) that we, as affiliates, will use to direct visitors to the merchant's website.

```
http://6cfb5nqj92o6g2jds8lyf9-tts.hop.clickbank.net/
```

Affiliate links come in different forms and carry different features, but they all identify one critical element – the affiliate who sent the visitor. This works via an **affiliate ID** on the link. Each affiliate ID inside the affiliate link is unique, and it identifies each affiliate seller. This enables many affiliate sellers to sell the same product while correctly keeping track of who gets the credit for the sales.

We use this unique affiliate link in all of our offers and marketing materials to promote the merchant's product. It identifies us as the referrer for the visitors and credits us for sales.

In some cases, the merchant gives you an affiliate code in URL format. You would know by the http:// or https:// it starts with. As you know by now, this is a URL – a website address, not a link. It's useful to gain a basic understanding of how to recognize and create a link in code (i.e., HTML) so that we can use affiliate links correctly.

*<a href="**http://www.thisIsTheDestinationWhenLinkIs Clicked.com/**">This is the text that would appear as the clickable link</a>*

That's the entire code, so include the < and > and the apostrophes. As you may have guessed, our URL-formatted affiliate code goes into the **http://www.thisIsTheDestinationWhen LinkIsClicked.com/** part. The text that you want to appear for the link goes in the **This is the text that would appear as the clickable link** part.

Doing so makes our affiliate code a clickable link – and this is the format of all links online. You can use the same structure to link to other pages and control the link text. All you need to do is change the destination URL (**http://www.thisIsTheDestinationWhen LinkIsClicked.com/**) and the link text (***This is the text that would appear as the clickable link***).

Step 4: Adopt the product's swipe files

Swipe file refers to a set of tested and proven sales letters and marketing materials. In Online Marketing, it is common practice for merchants to create ready-made swipe files for their products that their affiliates may use. On the one hand, this allows the merchants to control the message they want to spread regarding their products. On the other hand, swipe files make it easy for affiliates to sell the merchant's product.

Swipe files may include blog posts, press releases, and even a pre-written email series composed of multiple sequence emails. These swipe files have undergone testing and are proven to work. As an affiliate, we are free to use these swipe files to promote the merchant's product.

While we can use these swipe files for our promotional emails without alteration, always remember that we are not the only affiliate promoting this product. All affiliates will be given the use of the same generic materials.

The best way to maximize these swipe files is to edit them to fit our particular audience. We will be using these swipe files as templates to build from – don't simply copy and paste.

We are particularly interested in the product's email swipe files. We can find a product's swipe files from the product's affiliate resources. This **affiliate dashboard** is a page in the merchant's website dedicated to its affiliates.

If the merchant didn't set up an affiliate resource page, we could ask for swipe files directly from the merchant. Use the merchant's contact form or send them an email requesting the swipe files. We discussed how to find email addresses from the **Seed traffic method 6: Influencer outreach** section in Chapter 6.

The worst case scenario is that the merchant doesn't have any swipe files. In this case, we can use the product's sales page copy or product description as the basis for writing our sequence emails.

This is added work on our part, but if a product is truly desirable for selling to our audience, the added effort is worth it. We can follow the email writing structure that we discussed in the **Anatomy of powerful emails** section of Chapter 7.

Step 5: Send promotional emails to our audience

Once we've secured the email swipe files and adapted them to fit our audience, we can load these emails inside our nurture email series. Make sure that these promotional emails (emails that sell products) flow sensibly throughout the entire nurture email series. We don't want these promotional emails to come before the welcome email for example, or to veer off topic from the previous sequence email that our audience received from our email series.

By adding monetization to our automated nurture email series, we have now created a passive income machine.

Keep in mind that some products are available for sale over limited periods only. These products are on sale for a while; then the merchant pulls them out of the market – they may be seasonal, special product lines, or limited edition products. Sending our promotional emails as broadcasts are better options for these types of offers.

We can set our broadcast emails to send on a set schedule as well, so we don't have to manually load and send them on our target dates.

Remember to use, check, and test your unique affiliate link. Make sure that it works, and the click gets credited to your account. Our efforts go to waste if we are selling the products but others get credit for the sales and receive the commissions.

Create and Sell Our Own Product

While we can remain an affiliate and make lots of money doing so, creating and selling our own product is the dream. Creating our own product gives us control over the content and the price. Having our own product also lifts our credibility. We can also tailor-fit our product offerings to the exact needs of our audience.

We will enjoy more flexibility when promoting our own products vs. promoting as an affiliate. For example, most ad platforms don't allow promotion of affiliate products, but they will allow us to freely advertise our own products.

Creating and selling our own product is an entire topic of its own. This is a very rich field of discussion that won't fit in this chapter. The product creation topic ranges from manufacturing, sourcing, logistics – if we plan to create a tangible product – to writing, programming, and producing if we are producing a digital one. The way we go about creating our product depends on what type of product we want to sell.

However, there are principles in product creation that I can share with you that sit beyond the norm and will put you a cut above the rest.

Most product creators make a product out of what they know, or they emulate what's selling like hotcakes in the market. This is a good place to start, and use as a benchmark, for our product decisions. Although, consider that we have the added advantage of having an existing audience. We should maximize that resource. Here are two important tips that we should consider when creating a product.

Tip 1: Rely on our audience

When brainstorming for product creation, it's always wise to ask our audience for their ideas about what features and functionalities they want and need. From this audience feedback, create a minimum viable product (MVP) – a functional but bare-bones version (or early build) of the intended final product.

Whether it's a tangible product or a digital product, offer this early build version to the audience at a pre-launch price (i.e., heavily-discounted price) in exchange for feedback and an early look at the product.

We use this MVP version as a testing ground for our audience while encouraging them to send us their feedback, a practice called **beta-testing**.

Beta-testing allows us to test product response on real people, as well as develop the product in the right direction based on audience feedback.

Doing a beta test also gives us our early evangelists for the product. Beta-testers are great sources of case studies and testimonials that are useful in our product sales page when we launch.

Tip 2: Put extra effort on the sales page

The sales page is a big factor in determining if a product is going to sell or not.

It's smart to get started with a single sales page before risking resources in building more complicated modern funnels. We get to see modern techniques that use complicated sales funnels and video series to sell. However, the main principles of these funnels boil down to the same principles of a successful sales page.

Here are the critical components of any sales page that need special attention. Working on these helps us sell more of our products.

- **Headline.** The headline is a make-or-break component of any sales letter or marketing message. It catches the reader's limited attention and lures them in to read the rest of the copy. Our headlines must be brief, captivating, and curiosity-piquing, but also be accurate. We can add a kicker (a small snippet of text BEFORE the headline) and a sub-headline (a small snippet AFTER the headline) to add detail.

- **Body**. The body is the main part of the sales page copy showing the details of the offer. An effective structure to follow is to start with a product story that illustrates the pains, problems, and issues of the audience. Follow it up with "imagine if" scenarios that paint a picture of life when the problem gets resolved. After that, we insert our own story related to the product – a little background of ourselves plus how we discovered or used the product to great effect. The idea is to emphasize why our audience should listen to us, as well as make us relatable. We can then introduce the product itself, its features, and most importantly, its benefits.

- **Social proof**. Social proof – before and after pictures, client testimonials, professional credentials, media appearances, and influencer endorsements – strengthens our credibility and the credibility of our product.

- **Bonuses**. Bonuses (as long as they're relevant to the main product and are packed with quality) add value to our entire offer package. Bonuses, like free items or free shipping, are slowly becoming the norm, and most consumers expect it. List the normal product prices beside each bonus item to highlight the value of the entire bonus package.

- **Guarantee terms**. Similar to bonuses, most online transactions offer a "no questions asked" money-back guarantee or some form of risk-reversal, and buyers have come to expect this. Lay out your guarantee terms to assure the buyer that you confidently stand behind the quality of your product.

- **Call to action**. This is the part where we ask for the sale and provide the order button to facilitate the purchase process. Every effort put in our sales copy is wasted if we don't have the mechanism for visitors to make purchases. It's a great practice to include the summaries of the items, the benefits, and the guarantee terms along with the order button. A great persuasive tool to add is the "what if you do nothing?" scenario meant to make the visitor think seriously of the consequences should they not buy our product (i.e., continuous suffering of pain, persistence of the issue, non-resolution of the problem).

- **Images**. Place relevant images on major sections of the sales page copy. Images serve as emphasis tools, as well as visual breaks from the wall of gray that sales copy text can become. Images also improve the aesthetic value of the entire sales page.

- **Closing salutations**. We end our sales page copy with our sign-off phrase and signature. This is also a great opportunity to add a P.S. as a final call to action. Adding multiple post-scripts (i.e., P.S., P.P.S., and P.P.P.S.) is also a standard, and effective, practice.

Regardless of the form of sales letter we use – a single sales page, a sales funnel along multiple pages, or a video sales letter – these are the staple components of any sales page.

Stage 3 - Passive Income Machine: Wrap-Up and Pro Tips

Up to this point, we've been spending money, time, and effort building the foundations of a sustainable and lucrative business. It's only fair that we are rewarded for all of the hard work we've done to provide value for our niche crowd. We do this by offering premium, paid solutions to our audience. These solutions can either be our own products, or we can offer other merchants' solutions as an affiliate.

When integrating monetization into our Agile Online Income Machine, the guiding principle never changes – <u>keep providing value</u>.

With that in mind, we should be able to weave relevant and valuable offers into our existing relationship-building machine. This evolves our online business into a passive income machine.

When it comes to our passive income machine, here are a few good pointers to follow.

Tip 1: Start as an affiliate

This is worth repeating – starting as an affiliate allows us to earn money immediately – without the associated risks of creating our own product and the difficulty of handling customer support. It allows us to test and analyze the types of offers that resonate with our audience. Should we choose to create our own product in the future, we'll be more inclined to build a product that our audience is likely to buy.

Tip 2: Affiliate payment thresholds

Affiliate programs have payment threshold settings. Payment threshold refers to the minimum amount we need to accumulate before affiliate payment is released to us. Until we hit that amount, our affiliate commissions will stay in our account and carry over into the next payment period.

It's important to set the payment threshold to what works for your unique situation. Take into consideration the need for that money, as well as how consistent and fast are we generating sales to hit that threshold.

A good practice is to set a low threshold when starting out. This allows for more frequent payments but will incur more processing costs, if such costs apply. This will help us pay our expenses to run our business.

Once our sales grow and become more consistent, we can adjust the payment threshold to higher amounts. This lowers any applicable costs for processing and receiving our payments.

If there are no charges for each payment sent, we can set the threshold at the levels we want.

Tip 3: Test the affiliate link

We must make sure that our affiliate links are working properly after we generate them. We need to check if the link is live, redirecting people on click to the right destination page, and crediting us for the click. By extension, if we get credit for the click, we will also get credit for the sale.

Tip 4: Monitor affiliate links

Checking that our affiliate links work properly includes making sure they <u>keep working</u> properly. Make it a habit to ensure that our affiliate links are working and updated (once every two to three months is OK).

Most affiliate products are available for years (i.e., evergreen). However, there are merchants who pull their products off the market without notifying their affiliates. Monitoring our affiliate links is an effective way to prevent loss of profit should this happen. It also allows us to find a replacement affiliate product immediately.

For those affiliate offers that are time-sensitive or run for only a limited period, it's best to promote them with broadcast emails instead of integrating them into our nurture email series.

Now we have a working source of passive income. As we keep building on our Agile Online Income Machine, we can expect our income to grow at the same rate as we can grow our audience.

Take care of your audience and the income will take care of itself. Take action, and financial freedom will be within reach.

Chapter 9
Take the First Step in Faith

Putting Them All Together

*"All growth depends upon activity. There is
no development physically or intellectually
without effort, and effort means work." –
Calvin Coolidge*

Take Action and Keep Learning

We are now reaching the tail end of this book, and there's one truth that should dawn on us. It's the one epiphany that germinates deep inside everyone whenever a path of opportunity leads them face to face with the possibility of achieving their goals – the truth that nothing changes if we don't take action.

Earning income is not enough. We may fight through and conquer the pitfalls of employment, but retirement is a certainty we all need to face as we realize that financial independence alone can't save us. Financial freedom is the goal, and passive income is the mechanism towards it.

A financially free life will give us the money, time, and choice freedom to live the life of our dreams – on our own terms.

Realize also that financial freedom is no longer the exclusive domain of the business tycoons, real estate magnates, investment sages, and Network Marketing elites. With the right skills and unwavering grit, we can make money online and build an online passive income machine with none of the drawbacks of the classic passive income models.

All of these possibilities fit in the palms of our hands – this is financial freedom in a thumb drive.

Here's a bird's eye view of the entire Agile Online Income Machine and how all the components fit together.

Core Methodology: Step-by-Step Overview and Review

We've come a long way and discussed the core methodology of the Agile Online Income Machine in depth. It's a lot to take in. Here's a step-by-step overview to serve as a review and reference guide to help you take action and build your own online passive income business.

Core 1: Niche selection

- ***Step 1: Choose your niche***

    1. Brainstorm niche ideas.
    2. Filter through affinity validation.
    3. Filter through market validation.
    4. Break ties with tiebreaker filters (i.e., big three? + easy differentiation?).
    5. Choose one niche topic.

- ***Step 2: Gather niche intel***

    1. Research niche keywords.
    2. Research niche influencers.
    3. Research niche crowd.

Core 2: Audience-building machine component

- ***Step 3: Create your lead magnet***

    1. List down five of the most prominent niche crowd questions, struggles, problems, issues, and concerns.
    2. Find niche tools that solve these questions, struggles, problems, issues, and concerns.

3. Write the lead magnet (i.e., eReport featuring five niche tools).
4. Add enhancements (i.e., cover page, legal disclaimers, supporting images, conclusion/call to action).
5. Export as a PDF file.

- ***Step 4: Build your squeeze page***

    1. Secure your domain name.
    2. Subscribe to your web hosting service.
    3. Configure your domain's nameserver (DNS) settings in your domain registrar's (i.e., ***Namecheap.com***) settings to connect your domain name to your web hosting service.
    4. Install and configure Wordpress.
    5. Create a new page and use your content editor of choice (i.e., ***Thrive Themes*** – paid or ***Elementor*** – free) to build an enticing squeeze page for your lead magnet.
    6. Upload your lead magnet.

- ***Step 5: Incorporate your opt-in form***

    1. Subscribe to your email marketing app.
    2. Create a list inside the email marketing app.
    3. Initialize your agile email series (i.e., welcome email with lead magnet download link + trailing question email) inside the email marketing app.
    4. Integrate the opt-in form code to your squeeze page.

5. Test-run your funnel – *subscribe to your opt-in form* ➜ *double opt-in confirmation email arrives (applicable for double opt-in setup only)* ➜ *welcome email arrives with lead magnet download link* ➜ *lead magnet link is working and downloadable* ➜ *trailing question email arrives on the interval you set* ➜ *reply to your trailing question email* ➜ *reply email should arrive at intended inbox when you reply to the trailing question email.*

Core 3: Traffic generation

- ### *Step 6: Drive traffic to your squeeze page*

  1. Get the Agile Online Income Machine running by choosing a seed traffic method.
  2. Observe the community first. Take note of posts/activities that gain the most attention.
  3. Familiarize yourself with the community and slowly participate by posting.
  4. Make promotional posts that weave links to your squeeze pages (as applicable) alongside your regular posts.
  5. Extend to other communities and master this chosen seed traffic method.
  6. Explore and try other traffic methods, even those beyond the coverage of this book.

Core 4: Relationship-building machine component

- ### *Step 7: Build your nurture email series*

  1. Constantly send useful industry updates to your audience via broadcast emails while you're still building your nurture email series (i.e., currently only has welcome email + trailing question email). Follow your drip schedule.

2. Read audience replies to your trailing question emails.
3. Create sequence emails that answer your audience's inquiries. If the email gets too long, publish it as a blog post and link to it from the sequence email.
4. Integrate the new sequence email to the nurture email series. Follow your drip schedule.
5. Move the trailing question email at the end of the nurture email series. Edit the trailing question email accordingly, so it fits and makes sense along the nurture email series.

- ***Step 8: Build a relationship (know, like, and trust) and turn your audience into fans***

    1. Continue growing and extending your nurture email series.
    2. You can dial down your industry updates broadcast emails as your nurture email series gets longer.

Core 5: Passive income machine component

- ***Step 9: Monetize by offering affiliate solutions.***

    1. Wait for your audience size to reach 450-500.
    2. Find affiliate products that solve your fans' questions, struggles, problems, issues, and concerns.
    3. Choose great affiliate products to offer to your audience based on the product itself and the product's sales page.
    4. Generate your unique affiliate link. Test that it works and credits you for the click.
    5. Secure email swipe files and edit accordingly to create your promotional emails. Integrate your unique affiliate link.
    6. Send the promotional email to your fans. Weave it into the nurture email series as a sequence email if the flow fits. Otherwise, send as a broadcast email –

particularly if it's time-sensitive, a one-off, or doesn't fit the nurture email series flow.

- ***Step 10: Create and sell your own products.***

What Can We Do with Three Hours per Week?

If you can spare **three hours per week**, you have a chance of succeeding.

Listed here are the most productive tasks that we can do on our three hours per week.

Productive task 1: Keep generating traffic

Simply put, generating traffic to our website or our squeeze pages turns the key of the ignition and gets our online money-making engine started. Traffic also fuels our entire Agile Online Income Machine.

We can never have too much relevant traffic. The key word here is <u>relevant</u>.

If you have nothing else to do, generating traffic to your funnels is always a productive task to engage in.

Productive task 2: Continually extend our nurture email series

Our nurture email series is the mechanism that automates our relationship-building and money-making efforts. Setting up our relationship-building and promotional emails as sequence emails in an email series makes our make-money-online machine generate passive income. Achieving this level of automation frees up our time to live our lives and enjoy the activities we love.

Each sequence email we add in the email series is an autonomous agent that turns our audience into fans, and our fans into buyers, all on autopilot.

Writing valuable sequence emails and extending our nurture email series is always a productive activity. Keep growing the nurture email series by finding a good balance between valuable information and enticing offers.

Productive task 3: Write at least 200 words every day

Writing content is always a productive task. Even if you don't have the time to finish an entire article or email, getting into the habit of writing every day will serve you well.

It's reasonable to write 200 words over 30 minutes of focused writing. Once you acquire the discipline of writing daily, you'll have consistent material for traffic generation (i.e., guest posts, or community posts) or sequence emails for your nurture email series.

Working on these tasks diligently will grow your business continuously.

Improve Your Credibility and Exude Professionalism

Our name and the audience perception of our brand are the linchpins that determine whether we would generate sales and earn money. That's the reason why we have a relationship-building component inside our Agile Online Income Machine – to build trust and improve our brand image.

Beyond the nurture email series and the valuable broadcast emails that we send our audience, there are additional elements that can help us gain additional credibility and project professionalism – adopting **website credibility elements** and having a **custom email address**. Both of these simple tweaks can contribute a long way to creating a positive impact on our overall brand image.

Improvement 1: Website credibility elements

Our entire website, at this point, is bare bones. It only contains one single page – a squeeze page that serves as our front page.

Other elements can add credibility and professionalism to our website and our brand. These elements are present in every credible website, and visitors expect to see them in ours.

- **Element 1: About Us page**. The **About Us** page on our website tells visitors more about us. It speaks of our story, our skills, and our credentials.
- **Element 2: Contact Us page**. The **Contact Us** page gives our visitors information on how to reach us. It can contain the addresses to our social media pages, as well as a contact form for sending us messages. To create a contact form, we can install the ***Ninja Forms*** plugin (https://wordpress.org /plugins/ninja-forms/).
- **Element 3: Legal pages**. The legal pages include our website's **terms of service, privacy policy**, and any **disclaimers**. These pages are important to assure that we protect our visitors' rights. It also provides us with legal coverage should any issue arise. At the very least, have a **privacy policy**, since the law requires this. You can go to https://www.websitepolicies.com/ to help you get started with boilerplate website policies.
- **Element 4: Logo and Favicon**. Having a logo helps our brand become visually recognizable in an instant. We can use any image-editing tool to create our own logo or outsource it to a freelance designer. The **favicon** is that tiny icon that accompanies websites in browser tabs, desktop and app shortcuts, bookmarks, domain bar, etc. We can generate a favicon using this online tool – http://realfavicongenerator .net/. We can then upload this favicon to our website via going to the *WordPress dashboard* ➜ *Appearance* ➜ *Customize* ➜ *Site Identity* ➜ *Site Icon*.

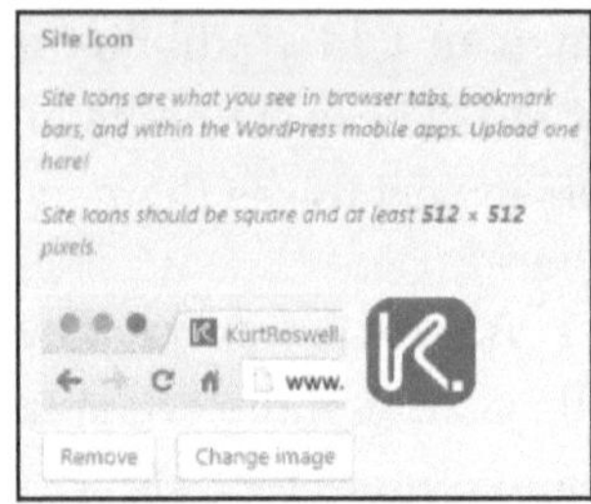

Notes for this section

- Never publish your email address on a public page.
  Otherwise, automated scrapers will catch it, and you will
  receive unwanted spam emails. If it's unavoidable, mask
  your email address from robots, at the very least. You can do
  this by writing your email as **myemail[at]mydomain
  .com** instead of straight up **myemail@mydomain.com**.
  Just add a note to your visitors to change the **[at]** to @.

Improvement 2: Custom email address

A **custom email address**, otherwise known as a **custom domain
email address**, is an email address that bears your own domain
name. Instead of having a generic webmail address like kurtroswell
@gmail.com or kurtroswell@yahoo.com, I can have an email address
like kurt@kurtroswell.com or contact@kurtroswell.com.

As a business and a brand, having a custom email address
projects credibility. People perceive businesses and brands that carry
their own domain name on their email addresses as professional.

- **Step 1: Create a custom email address.** Since we
  already have our own domain name as well as a web hosting
  service, we already have the groundwork for a custom email
  address. It's only a simple setup from here.

  1. Log in to your web hosting account (not your domain
     registrar). If you followed the recommendation I
     made here, that would be *SiteGround* (web hosting
     service), and not *Namecheap* (domain registrar).

2. Log in to the **cPanel** of your web hosting account.

3. In your cPanel dashboard, go to *Mail* ➜ *Email Accounts*.

4. Enter your preferred email address. **contact@**, **info@**, and **<yourfirstname>@** are common email addresses. Also, make sure you're attaching it to the correct domain name.

5. Type your password for this particular email account. Take note and remember this.

6. Click on *Create Account* and you're done.

7. You can access and read your emails by going to http://www.YOURDOMAIN.com/webmail and logging in with the username/email address and password.

- **Step 2: Receive and send emails inside Gmail.** Accessing our custom email address using the interface I mentioned above may be inconvenient. We may be used to reading emails from our favorite email inbox.
  With a simple set up, we can receive emails sent to our custom email address while also sending out emails from the same address, all the while still using our favorite email inbox. We'll use **Gmail** as an example since it's the most widely used.

  1. To receive emails inside your Gmail inbox, log in to Gmail.

  2. Click the *Settings*. It's inside the cog-like button on the top right.

  3. Select *Accounts and Import* ➜ *Check mail from other accounts:* ➜ *Add a mail account*.

  4. Enter your custom email address in the *email address:* input field. Choose *Import emails from my other account (POP3)* in the next window then click *Next*.

  5. Fill in the *Username* and *Password*. Leave the rest at default settings, unless you know what you're

doing. If you encounter an error, try using your entire custom email address (i.e., include the @yourdomainname .com) as your *Username*. Click on *Add Account*.

6. Gmail will ask if you want to be able to send mail as your custom email address. Choose *yes* and click *Next*.

7. Fill up the name (i.e., what the recipient will see in their *from:* field) for this account. <u>UNCHECK</u> the *treat as an alias* setting. Click *Next Step*.

8. Fill in the *Username* and *Password* for this custom email address account. Again, use the entire custom email address as the *Username* if you get an error. Leave the other settings at default.

9. You then need to access your custom email address to verify with Gmail that you own the account. Go to <u>http://www.YOURDOMAIN.com/webmail</u>.

10. Log in to your custom email address account. Find the verification email sent by Gmail.

11. Click on the link inside the verification email or copy the code in Gmail to verify.

12. Congratulations! You can now receive and send emails to and from your custom email address within Gmail.

<u>Notes for this section</u>

- When composing emails inside Gmail, be sure to check the **From** field. Select (using the drop-down arrow on the side) the custom email address you intend to use.

Conclusion

We have now reached the conclusion of **Financial Freedom in a Thumb Drive: The Millennial's Guide to Building Passive Income Online**.

I would like to thank you for your support and wish you all the best on your financial freedom journey. I hope I was able to provide you with crucial information, an inspiring path, or even just that glimmer of hope you need to take a legitimate shot at getting out of your rat race.

We're already at the end of this book, but our entwined paths continue. I'm very invested in your success and financial freedom. I believe that the more of us reach financial freedom (with no money and time worries), the more of us can pursue our true purpose and contribute to this world in a meaningful way.

If you have any success stories, suggestions, or inquiries, I invite you to reach out to me via these channels.

- Website: https://www.kurtroswell.com/
- Email: contact@kurtroswell.com
- Facebook: https://www.facebook.com/kurtroswell/
- Twitter: https://www.twitter.com/kurtroswell/

I will try to respond to your queries with the best of my abilities. I may not be able to answer all the messages, but rest assured that I will read them all.

One last piece of advice, if you start earning substantial income from your Online Marketing machine, diversify. Diversification may mean building another online business in another niche topic or pursuing another financial freedom vehicle altogether.

While the Agile Online Income Machine model of making money online is as stable as they come, there's always uncertainty when it comes to the future of businesses. *Yahoo!* was the titan of the online world just a decade ago, and now it's a cautionary tale. *Twitter* used to be the darling of Silicon Valley. Now it's stagnant with no investors giving it a serious second look.

The fact is, no matter how strong your business is at any given point, it can tumble in a heartbeat. This is truer online, where new ideas, game-changing developments, and disruptive technologies enter the space daily. The more streams of income you have in place, the more stable and secure your financial freedom status will be.

Making money online opens the door to the greatest upside and financial returns vis-a-vis capital and time requirements, especially when compared to the classic financial freedom vehicles. Online Marketing is, without a doubt, the best place to start. Take advantage of that and build a stable financial freedom portfolio.

Remember that our greatest and most stable asset is not our businesses, not our real estate properties, and not our investment portfolios. All of these are affected by market forces and, thus, are fragile by nature.

Our greatest asset is our confidence in our ability to create something from nothing. In that sense, we know that we can always build from scratch, even if everything we've created is taken away from us.

This is what **Financial Freedom in a Thumb Drive** gives you – the skills for creating valuable assets from thin air and the ability to make money online building from scratch.

Time to do some #adulting. Time to get to work. Time to be financially free.

This is your time.

To your successful financial freedom journey,
Kurt Roswell

> *"Vision without action is a daydream.*
> *Action without vision is a nightmare." –*
> *Japanese Proverb*